EBBF
Ethical Business Building the Future

HOW

you can contribute

to a more prosperous, just & sustainable organization

THE BOSS BOOKS

HOW YOU CAN CONTRIBUTE TO A MORE PROSPEROUS, JUST & SUSTAINABLE ORGANIZATION
EBBF – ethical business bulding the future

Edited and published by The Boss Books/Libri d'Impresa Edizioni

One Hour Marketing Srl
Via Torino 9, 21013 – Gallarate (VA), Italy
www.thebossbooks.com

THE BOSS BOOKS

ISBN 9791280622976

Contents

PREFACE
Daniel Truran

Ethical business building the future... but how?

Daniel Truran

—

Strategist, impact innovator, speaker, enabler and business schools professor. Director General of the ebbf, co-founder Impact Hub, Madrid. B Corp Ambassador. Partner at NOW Partners

"At this critical juncture in history, the advancement of civilization entails the construction of a global social order, based on a profound consciousness of the oneness of humanity, in which justice is the central organizing principle, and the well-being and prosperity of all peoples is pursued."

The Conceptual Framework
by the Institute for Studies in Global Prosperity

Could the new rules of the game be based on century old wisdom?

I have been serving this ebbf global community since 2001. Every year I benefitted from mindset changing, surprising, deeply inspiring conversations with members of this community. This has been both a source of joy and inspiration but also of frustration. Why are so few people able to be immersed in this mind evolving, life changing, deep understanding of how the world is and how it should be?

This is why we wrote this book. For you to gain at least a glance of some of the insights, ideas, actions, questions coming from the direct experience of ebbf members. Showing the many ways in which these ethical people ARE building the future.

The world is "begging" for what seems to be so hard to see around us: hope and fresh new perspectives of the future we can create, together.

We live at a complex crossroads where certainty is no longer a reality. It is also a unique time where we understand that living with the same mindset of the past no longer serves us.

A time where we are able to build and evolve with a transformational speed like never before.

However, conversations with ebbf members have allowed an unexpected insight to emerge. We have learnt that if we want the best kind of progress to occur, action should not be the first step.

Before action, we should try to understand.

Using the luxury of taking the time to pause and really understand what is happening around us. What are the fundamentals of the new world economic system we want to build. Time to explore together some of the most useful trends of a new system that are already emerging.

It is human nature to try to understand, to want to know what happens next.

Too many are looking for band-aid short term patches because of the need to make sense of what surrounds us.

This book moves away from the superficial "here are three steps to achieve progress" and introduces you to a wider mindset of abundance.

The uncertainty and fear of the future vanishes when you are surrounded by others who are living these times in a fresh new way. The diversity of the personal experiences you will read in this book will open your mind in just how many opportunities for a new evolved economic system are now possible and how to harness them.

In these chapters you will be able to come into contact with some of the humans who have inspired and keep inspiring me and my life.

Ebbf members featured in this book have the ability to not just carefully observe, deeply reflect to understand the fundamentals of the progress we need.

These are people from around the world who are actually openly exploring actions, based on reflection and a sense of responsibility and a desire to ... build the future.

The energy of being surrounded by leaders like the authors of these chapters is contagious.

People who, each in their own special way, have decided to become protagonists of the change that is needed. People who see the only way forward as an individual volition but moved forwad in a collective action as part of communities of change that put the capacity building of each individual at the centre of progress.

I have observed many inspiring leaders fail when they, heroically, decide to lead the change that is needed. Building the community with which not only change, but deep learning and growth can be achieved is where the stories of ebbf leaders differ and have enriched my life.

"... developing a culture which promotes a way of thinking, studying, and acting, in which all consider themselves as treading a common path of service – supporting one another and advancing together, respectful of the knowledge that each one possesses at any given moment and avoiding the tendency to divide the believers into categories such as deepened and uninformed – is an accomplishment of enormous proportions. And therein lie the dynamics of an irrepressible movement."

Ridvan 2010

Another common trait of ebbf members and authors of this book is that they are explorers, not experts.

They are in a constant open observation, a desire to discover how. So much so that ebbf's podcast is titled: ethical business building the future, discovering how.

This is the spirit that guides this Baha'i-inspired global learning community of leaders in the most diverse fields, positions, geographical spread. The desire to consult, understand, then try out new things, explore new paths and then go back to learning.

People who are then finding and exploring new and better ways to have the individual find unity in community-led initiatives.

We hope that the stories you will read will open new insights into how many opportunities we have to walk our own paths, with others, to harness the emerging new world order that is taking over from a crumbling old world order that has pushed us, people and the planet beyond its limits.

What surprises me most about ebbf members?

Their optimism and their desire to serve others.

How they live with the curiosity of someone who knows something and wants to learn a lot.

With the intelligent humbleness of constantly being in discovery mode.

With the common ultimate goal of learning with others, of actively sharing, of smart and generous collaborative ways forward.

Moving away from the ego of being leaders whilst ignited by the personal responsibility to act.

"Efforts to build capacity fall short if arrangements are not swiftly made to accompany individuals into the arena of service. An adequate level of support extends far beyond encouraging words. When preparing to take on an unfamiliar task, working alongside a person with some experience increases consciousness of what is possible. An assurance of practical help can give a tentative venturer the courage to initiate an activity for the first time. Souls then advance their understanding together, humbly sharing the insights each possesses at a given moment and eagerly seeking to learn from fellow wayfarers on the path of service. Hesitation recedes and capacity develops to the point where an individual can carry out activities independently and, in turn, accompany others on the same path."

Universal House of Justice, Letter to the Continental Board of Counsellors, 29 Dec. 2015

ABOUT THE AUTHOR

Daniel Truran excels in guiding organizations towards achieving meaningful success and ethical purpose with his expertise in values-based leadership and business. He crafts strategic plans from complex scenarios and fosters adaptive, trust-based teams, connecting them to their core values and a global network of like-minded entities. With nearly 30 years of experience, including roles at Lush Europe, NESI Forum, and as co-founder of Impact Hub Madrid, he significantly contributes to social entrepreneurship and ethical business practices. As Director General of ebbf and a B Corp Ambassador, plus teaching roles at EOI Business School, ESADE, and Instituto Empresa, Daniel champions social innovation and ethical action. Holding a BA in Management Science, he's multilingual and resides in Madrid, dedicated to enhancing global well-being and prosperity.

Beyond Your Values Statement: Bringing Organizational Values to Life

Layli Miller-Muro

—

Layli Miller-Muro supports leaders and organizations working to operationalize their values, foster inclusive cultures, and prosper with purpose

"If the moral precepts and foundations of divine civilization become united with the material advancement of man, there is no doubt that the happiness of the human world will be attained and that from every direction the glad tidings of peace upon earth will be announced."

'Abdu'l-Bahá,
The Promulgation of Universal Peace

VALUES AS CORE

The economic and moral influence of corporations is vast. According to Global Justice Now, 79% of the world's 200 richest entities are corporations (21% are governments). This places a great economic and moral responsibility on companies to address societal challenges. From climate change to public health crises, companies have shown they have the reach and responsibility to act as agents of change. Their deep understanding of global interdependence also uniquely positions them to respond to international crises, such as supply chain and food shortages triggered by conflict or the rippling effects of a pandemic. Values-based business practices are a necessity in today's world, where stakeholders from all sectors demand transparency, accountability, and sustainability.

The pursuit of values-based business practices is a journey toward not only economic prosperity but also the creation of a world that values human dignity, environmental stewardship, and social equity. The "why" is clear: to build a future where profit is grounded in a purpose that honors our shared humanity and wellbeing of the planet. The "how" involves a committed process of embedding our highest values into the DNA of our organizations, ensuring that every decision, policy, and action reflects a deep commitment to principle.

Organizational culture is the reflection of a company's values in action, serving as an organization's guidepost that leads behavior and aspirations. The infusion of values into the organizational fabric is not just a mark of identity but the lifeblood of a thriving corporate culture and a forerunner of success. These values should provide a standard, and be evident not just in grand statements but in the day-to-day – the systems, policies, and the actions of leadership and staff. They should be lofty enough to inspire yet pragmatic enough to be understood and acted upon, with clear accountability measures woven into the continuous improvement process.

9 Reasons Why Values Are Important

Values, when translated into actions, will:

1. Create a clear and unified purpose for the company
2. Define your company's external brand and identity
3. Guide how your company does business
4. Influence the level of trust and integrity you hold
5. Attract talent and ensure inclusion
6. Obtain trust from stakeholders
7. Attract investors and funders
8. Inform the impact your company will have on the world
9. Support profitability and success

THE DISCREPANCY BETWEEN PROFESSED AND PRACTICED VALUES

Three out of four companies will fail in their efforts to be successful. Those that succeed have effective leadership that is able to set the course, map strategy, define goals, and bring together the right team to steer the organization forward. How leaders embody the company's values – their 'rules of the road' – dictates whether they'll remain on course, honor ethical considerations, and observe the laws and regulations in spirit and letter.

The stark reality is that while 90% of companies have values statements, only 27% of employees believe in their company's values and 24% have detailed what behaviors are expected in order to live their valuesvalues (Leadership IQ, April 17, 2022). This discrepancy between professed and practiced values is not a mere oversight; it is a chasm that can determine whether a company will flourish or flounder. It also impacts whether a company advances societal progress or simply extracts profit for personal gain without regard to its impact on people and the planet.

THE EVOLUTION OF CORPORATE PURPOSE

The evolution of companies towards a higher purpose than profit alone has been steady. In 1962, Nobel Laureate Milton Friedman, asserted that corporate social responsibility is a "fundamentally subversive doctrine" and that "there is one and only one social responsibility of business – to use its resources and engage in activities designed to increase its profits..." (Milton Friedman, Capitalism and Freedom, 1962). The laws of the time, upholding shareholder primacy, echoed this sentiment.

The narrative has shifted dramatically in recent years. In 2019, the Business Roundtable, which is the most influential organization of businesses in the United States, adopted a new Statement on the Purpose of a Corporation. The statement was signed by 181 CEO's of America largest companies. The statement acknowledged that its previous statements on corporate purpose "has stated that corporations exist principally to serve their shareholders" but "[it] has become clear that this language on corporate purpose does not accurately describe the ways in which we and our fellow CEO's endeavor every day to create value for all our stakeholders, whose long term interests are inseparable. We therefore provide the following statement on the purpose of a corporation which supersedes previous roundtable statements and more accurately reflects our commitment to a free market economy that serves all Americans."

In 2020, more than 3,000 global leaders, including 53 heads of state, along with corporate and NGO leaders convened in Davos at the World Economic Forum. They went further and affirmed "stakeholder capitalism," directly rejecting "shareholder or profit only capitalism." Specifically, they issued "The Davos Manifesto 2020," which states that "The purpose of a company is to engage all its stakeholders in shared and sustained value creation. In creating such value, a company serves not only its shareholders, but all its stakeholders – employees, customers, suppliers, local communities and society at large." This evolution is particularly exhilarating for someone like myself, who transitioned from corporate law to human rights advocacy. To witness these once-divergent spheres converge is to see the promise of a new corporate ethos where the value of a company is intertwined with the values it upholds.

THE CHALLENGES OF SHAPING VALUES

What does it mean to live by one's values? Values are the compass that guide us, the principles that drive a person's decisions and actions. While no one is perfect in upholding their values at all times, it's the conscious effort to live by them that shapes effective leadership. Our values define us, especially when they are tested, when we face the hard choices that may require sacrificing profit or personal gain.

Upon graduating from law school, I established an organization called the Tahirih Justice Center, which provides free holistic legal services for women and girls fleeing human rights abuses. Initially, I served on its board of directors and supported the organization's growth to a start-up size while maintaining a full-time job at a corporate law firm. After a few years, I joined its staff and became its Executive Director, leading the organization's growth over 20 years from a start-up to a well-established award-winning model of non-profit management.

Tahirih grew at a rapid pace and, at its peak had a total budget of $22M and 120 staff in five offices throughout the United States. The growth was both exhilarating and challenging. As we scaled up, I saw firsthand how the intimacy of a small organization easily fostered values alignment. We were a close-knit team, learning from each other almost by osmosis, with values discussions happening naturally, directly influenced by my own leadership and proximity.

But as we expanded, the organic conversations that once effortlessly knitted our values into the fabric of our workday began to unravel.

New systems and processes, particularly in decision-making, emerged as staff numbers swelled. The intuitive grasp of our core values that had once felt like second nature was slipping through our fingers. It was time to rein in and strategize, to intentionally cement clarity and accountability into the very walls of our growing institution.

I recall the episode with a high-profile leader who joined us – her credentials were impeccable. But her approach, borne from her tenure at established institutions, clashed with our culture. Accustomed to making unilateral decisions, she brought a top-down methodology alien to our ethos of consultative decision-making, sparking resistance. It wasn't an isolated case; we welcomed two such leaders from renowned institutions, tasked to steward operations, including finance and HR. Accustomed to the 'I'm the expert' approach, their top-down decision-making stirred unrest, a stark contrast to our culture of inclusivity and collective reasoning.

This highlighted the need to crystalize and integrate a culture of consultation within our performance evaluation system to prevent unilateral decision-making and ensure that everyone affected by decisions – or those with relevant information – was involved, reflecting our 'three eyes' rubric of inclusion (involving in the decision-making process those who are informed, those who will *implement*, and those who are *impacted*). Yet, here we were, watching this new approach steamroll over our practice of consultation. I remember those difficult conversations, where I stood firm on our culture and values, only to be met with resistance, a pushback that reflected a clear disconnect.

Then came the moment of truth during a new staff orientation. As I spoke of our nonpartisan ethos, articulating examples of collaboration across the political spectrum, I saw faces contort, skepticism bubble up. One new hire went so far as to declare that working with certain political affiliations was a violation of her personal values. That was a watershed moment. It wasn't just about who we were hiring, but also about how effectively we were communicating and embodying our values. It was evident; our operations had grown too complex for ad-hoc value alignment.

We needed structures – sophisticated, robust systems that could uphold our consultative decision-making and hold us accountable to the values we hold dear. It wasn't enough to declare our values; we had to live them, breathe them, and weave them into every layer of our organizational tapestry. During my tenure as CEO of the Tahirih Justice Center, I spearheaded the crafting of a process operationalize our values. It was an intricate journey; our organization was sprawling across the United States with a staff of 120, where a significant majority, 95%, did not know the spiritual principles inspired by the Bahá'í faith, yet the ethos of our organization was deeply rooted in it. I faced a pivotal transition as a leader, and it became crystal clear: the organization could not solely depend on my direct influence to infuse the Bahá'í-inspired principles. These values needed to be ingrained within the fabric of our organization – woven into its very structure and culture.

And so, we began the painstaking yet vital work of realigning, recalibrating, and restructuring. We embarked on an intensive strategic endeavor to operationalize our values, learning and adapting through every stage of this journey. What emerged was a distilled essence of our dedicated efforts, a set of practices and methodologies to ensure our values were more than just words – they were actions and commitments that defined us.

We fortified our approach, ensuring that every action was in harmony with our declared values – making it abundantly clear what we stand for and, just as importantly, what we stand against.

THE CORPORATE CULTURE CLASH: OPERATIONALIZING VALUES

Ensuring that the values of an organization are fully operationalized and shared by the people within it is critical to a thriving culture and the success of a company. Operationalizing values is a task laden with discomfort, requiring us to continually grow, learn, and improve. It demands time, resources, and the willingness to make sacrifices. Yet the endeavor is invaluable. When we align our journey with our values, we achieve more than success; we leave an indelible, positive imprint on society.

Evidence from over a thousand firms in the Great Places to Work database shows a strong positive link between an organization's financial success and its employees' belief in the practice of its proclaimed values. Effectively operationalizing a company's values increases indeed economic performance: a study from +1,000 firms reveals a strong correlation between financial performance and the extent to which employees believe their company's espoused values are practiced.

Specifically, employees are:

- 115% more engaged when their organization has a **well defined set of company values**
- 135% more engaged if their company always **hires people who fit their company values**
- 107% more engaged when their company has detailed **what specific behaviors are necessary to live their company values**

For most companies, values lack connections to documented behaviors, leadership accountability, performance appraisals, and hiring qualities; factors that, if executed well, could create a twofold increase in employee engagement. According to Leadership IQ, only a quarter of organizations specify the behaviors that align with their values, and even fewer – 21% – integrate these into performance reviews, despite a clear link to higher employee satisfaction. A mere 20% of companies consistently hire individuals who align with their values, although doing so could boost employee commitment. Accountability also appears to be lacking, with only a third of employees confident that their managers enforce value adherence. The deeper implications of these findings are reinforced by another study, revealing just 23% of U.S. employees feel empowered to apply their organization's values daily, and only 27% truly believe in them.

So how do we ensure values are more than just platitudes? How do we operationalize them? How do we invite employees to embrace a certain ethics? Everything begins with defining values, then aligning them with competencies, and setting expectations for behavior. We must employ a rigorous filter for our actions and choices, from hiring to partnerships and product launches. We must continuously orient and reorient our people around these values, reinforce them through rituals and recognition, and, critically, enforce them with accountability.

HOW TO MAKE YOUR VALUES ACTIONABLE

The process of operationalizing values is a continuous one that starts with identifying values, then involves filtering for values, orienting for values, reinforcing values, and enforcing values. This systematic approach to embedding organizational values -- following the five-step process of defining, filtering, orienting, reinforcing, and enforcing -- is perpetual and forms the heart of a company.

1. DEFINE. In Stage 1, the objective is to crystallize and refine the company's core values, pinpointing and enhancing areas to better represent the organization's mission. This involves engaging leadership and staff to evaluate and upgrade current values, assessing their application within the organization, and finalize a comprehensive values statement. Then, the values statement is further clarified to detail competencies and specific behaviors that reflect those values. The stage also includes developing a communication strategy to share these values with all stakeholders and creating an action plan to integrate the values across company functions, ensuring accountability is maintained.

- Define your high-level values.
- Define specific values competencies and behaviors.
- Define what your values mean you won't do.
- Share your values definitions (internally and externally).

2. FILTER. This stage involves scrutinizing people, projects, products, policies, procedures, and practices to ensure they resonate with the company's established values. It requires filtering out or filtering in the right elements, critical to an organization's success, to ensure values alignment. This stage can be difficult and involve hard decisions about withdrawing from projects, declining opportunitities, or parting ways with people.

- Hire staff that embody values.
- Choose projects and products based on values alignment.
- Decline opportunities that do not align with values.

3. ORIENT. Orientation is centered on educating employees and other stakehodlers about core values through training and workshops, ensuring that these principles are a living part of the organizational culture. It extends to onboarding, urging leaders to model these values, and establishing procedures for initiating value-consistent projects.

- Include values training in new hire orientation.
- Educate stakeholders on values.
- Include a values audit in project launch processes.

4. REINFORCE. Reinforcement is about acknowledging and celebrating employees who live out the company values, integrating these principles into performance evaluations, and maintaining a cycle of feedback and communication to keep the values at the forefront of organizational practices.

- Regularly train on values and competencies.
- Integrate values in performance evaluations.
- Report on values adherence.
- Celebrate models of living values.
- Publicize values.

5. ENFORCE. The enforcement phase is an ongoing commitment to monitoring and upholding the values, establishing accountability for lapses, and reporting on the organization's adherence to its value system, ensuring that values are not just aspirational but a concrete part of the company's operational ethos.

- Hold leadership and staff accountable.
- Quickly intercept or disengage when values aren't aligned.
- Conduct regular org-wide values assessments.
- Examine external perception of lived values.

CASE STUDY—PATAGONIA

Patagonia, the outdoor apparel company, is a prime example of a business that has successfully operationalized its core values. Established in 1973 by Yvon Chouinard, it has garnered acclaim for its environmental sustainability efforts and corporate responsibility deeply embedded in the company ethos.

INTERNAL CULTURE

Employee empowerment: Patagonia fosters a culture of shared decision-making. Employees have a say in product development, environmental initiatives, and company policies. This fosters a sense of ownership and aligns employee behavior with company values.

Work-life balance: Patagonia encourages employees to pursue outdoor activities. A generous paid time off policy and on-site childcare facilities enable employees to achieve a healthy work-life balance, reducing burnout and promoting employee well-being.

Activism as a core value: Patagonia actively supports environmental causes. From donating a percentage of sales to environmental groups to filing lawsuits against environmentally destructive practices, the company translates its values into action.

EXTERNAL PRODUCTS AND BRAND

Focus on durability: Patagonia builds products designed to last a lifetime. This reduces waste and aligns with the company's commitment to environmental responsibility. They offer a robust repair program, encouraging customers to fix their worn Patagonia gear instead of replacing it.

Environmentally conscious materials: Patagonia prioritizes recycled materials and organic cotton throughout their product line, minimizing their environmental footprint.

Transparency and advocacy: Patagonia is open about its supply chain and the environmental impact of its products. They actively advocate for sustainable practices and environmental protection, influencing the entire outdoor apparel industry.

IMPACT

Patagonia's focus on values has led to several positive outcomes:

High employee satisfaction: Patagonia consistently ranks high in "best places to work" lists due to its employee-centric approach.

Brand loyalty: Customers resonate with Patagonia's values, leading to strong brand loyalty and customer advocacy.

Reduced environmental impact: Patagonia's commitment to sustainability minimizes their footprint and sets an example for other businesses.

CONCLUSION

Patagonia's success demonstrates that integrating core values into daily operations is not just beneficial for society and the environment; it's also good for business. By prioritizing employee well-being, environmental responsibility, and product quality, Patagonia has built a loyal customer base and a thriving company culture. Their model serves as a roadmap for businesses aiming to live their values and achieve a positive impact.

CHALLENGING QUESTIONS

- How can you ensure your organization's values transcend rhetoric and become integral to every aspect of your operations?
- In what ways do you, as a leader or team member, actively contribute to embedding these values into your company's DNA?
- Can you identify a time when your company's actions truly mirrored its stated values? What was the impact internally and externally?
- How does your organization measure the effectiveness of its values in daily decision-making processes? Are there systems in place to hold individuals accountable?
- Reflecting on the example of the Tahirih Justice Center, what steps can you take to transform challenges into opportunities for strengthening your organization's value alignment?

ABOUT THE AUTHOR

Layli Miller-Muro is an internationally recognized social impact executive and purpose-driven thought leader. She is currently a Principal at Miller-Muro Consulting where through consulting, coaching, and training, she supports organizations, efforts to turn values-driven platitudes into practice. Trained as a corporate attorney, Layli served as CEO of the Tahirih Justice Center for 20 years, which she scaled to $22M with 120 staff in five offices, to protect women from human rights abuses. Layli was included in Goldman Sachs's inaugural list of the Top 100 Most Intriguing Entrepreneurs *and named by Newsweek Magazine as one of the 150 Most Fearless Women in the World.*

Scaling Up and Staying True: Engineering Systems with Ethical Foundations

Salim Afshar MD

—

Investor, Co-Founder,
Chief Medical & Innovation Officer
Reveal HealthTech Harvard Faculty

"Culture eats strategy for breakfast."

Peter Drucker

THE IMMUNE SYSTEM OF AN ORGANISATION

In my journey through the healthcare industry as either a surgeon, researcher, or entrepreneur, I've often been reminded of the broader context in which all businesses operate. Today, we find ourselves in an era of profound uncertainty. The very foundations that once offered stability to countless individuals are now quaking beneath our feet. Jobs, which served as steadfast anchors for many, are now in turbulent waters, constantly threatened by disruption. Artificial Intelligence has intensified these fears, with many worrying about the displacement of their roles. Goldman Sachs estimates that AI could potentially replace the equivalent of 300 million full-time jobs[1]. These fears are penetrating the minds of the young, with 69% of college graduates stating that they are worried that they will lose their jobs to AI[2]. But it's not just the economic landscape that's shifting. The moral compass that once united societies is now under strain. Common values and norms, the very glue that held communities together, are being questioned, leading to deeply divided societies. In the U.K., 61% of young people believe that moral values are on the decline, reflecting a global trend where younger generations perceive a shift in societal morals[3]. This fragmentation of our societies has eroded the empathy and compassion we once held for one another. Conversations, which should be bridges of understanding, have become minefields. Misunderstandings arise, not necessarily from the words spoken, but from the underlying tensions that individuals carry with them – be it from family, societal pressures, or other external forces.

1. https://www.bbc.com/news/technology-65102150
2. https://www.tidio.com/blog/ai-trends/
3 https://gitnux.org/moral-decline-statistics/

Studies in social psychology have shown that individuals under high levels of stress are more likely to misinterpret social cues and react with heightened sensitivity. For instance: I make a casual remark, and you, perhaps due to stresses unrelated to our conversation, respond with unexpected severity. Such interactions, fueled by external pressures and personal triggers, lead to conflicts, both within the workplace and outside. And as any seasoned entrepreneur or professional knows, when pressure mounts, breakdowns are inevitable. Those pressure-induced breakdowns ultimately result in increased turnover rates, decreased employee engagement, and a toxic culture. Even large companies, despite their vast resources and structures, are as susceptible to these pressures, highlighting the need for proactive measures to address the impact of external stressors and their unintended consequences internally.

In this era marked by uncertainty, businesses face a dual mandate: to grow (swiftly) such that they can achieve their impact goals and to do so ethically. Rapid expansion provides team members with a reassuring anchor, but it's the ethical underpinning that ensures meaningful impact. This ethical commitment goes beyond just products; it shapes the very culture of a company, fostering unity as a principle and facilitating open dialogue. When businesses place people at the heart of operations, they create environments where individuals can flourish, both professionally and personally. Moreover, the positive ripple effects of a harmonious work culture can extend beyond the confines of the office. Just as societal patterns can influence workplace dynamics, a positive work environment can influence society at large. The skills and values nurtured within the workplace – teamwork, understanding, and empathy – can be mirrored in our interactions with family and friends. In essence, **by fostering ethical and successful businesses, we are sowing the seeds for a more cohesive and compassionate society**.

As a doctor, I like to compare the culture of an organization with that of the human immune system. Just as a robust immune system protects our health, a strong organizational culture safeguards the internal dynamics and shields against external threats.

"A strong organizational culture safeguards the internal dynamics and shields against external threats, just like a robust immune system protects our health".

In addition, when a threat does penetrate the human body, the immune system quickly responds both locally and at a system level to contain and resolve the threat. Similarly, a strong organizational culture will quickly respond to organizational challenges and bypass system blockages enabling clear communication and action across the entire system. So how do we develop this culture, and more importantly, how do we do this at scale? Start with seeing the end in the beginning. Reverse engineering what it will take to have a healthy and functioning culture that is both preventative and appropriately responsive to the needs of the individuals and organization. As organizations are comprised of individuals, start by envisioning the desired outcome: a cohesive organization where every individual values reflection, action, and a questioning mindset. While newcomers might initially prioritize self-promotion, the ingrained culture should guide them towards collective growth. If they resist this evolution, they might not be the right fit. Some companies, such as Zappos, implemented a policy called "Pay to Quit", offering new employees $2,000 to leave if they felt unhappy at the company, filtering out individuals not aligned with the company culture. This is just one instrument that can be used, but one must go beyond instruments and incentives. Even with a strong foundation, continuous efforts must be made at all levels, from management to the board, to maintain this culture, ensuring that as the company grows, its core values remain unshaken.

Before going into what this practically means let's look at the key principles behind it.

KEY PRINCIPLES

In the heart of every successful company lies a commitment to coherence and the recognition of the human spirit. These twin pillars not only shape internal dynamics but also define how the world perceives the organization.

- **Coherence** is the cornerstone of a company's reputation. When an organization functions harmoniously, it resonates in its products and services, creating an inherent trust with its consumers. Just as Apple meticulously crafted its products, ensuring every detail aligned with its vision, companies must ensure that their internal values are consistently reflected externally. This authenticity can't be manufactured; it must be genuinely lived by its members.

- On the other hand, **allowing employees to be human** is equally vital. In a world driven by metrics and bottom lines, it's essential to remember the human element. By fostering an environment where employees can express compassion, empathy, and genuine connection, companies not only enhance their internal culture but also project these values outwardly. In addition, there are unintended consequences that can be positive, from identifying capabilities that were overlooked, as well as ideas and innovation driven by curiosity and creativity which only occurs when there is space made for employees to be human. This human touch, combined with coherence, forms the foundation of an organization set up for success.

Now let's explore a method built on these principles.

REVERSE ENGINEERING: THE METHOD

To build a sustainable and dynamic culture within an organization, especially one that is rapidly growing, it is crucial to focus on three main steps: Mindset, Action, and Reflection and Learning.

Step 1: Mindset

The mindset of the leaders and employees drives the behaviour and actions within the organization. It is essential to be intentional about the mindset, setting a positive tone, and transforming people through a clear vision. This proactive approach helps in instilling the values and culture in the minds of others as the business grows. However, it is common for organizations to show signs of strain when they reach a certain scale. This is where many fall into the trap of trying to improve culture using compensatory methods like traditional budgeting and rewards structures, which can lead to negative consequences. Instead, leaders should focus on adjusting their mindset, reflecting on guiding principles, and ensuring that their actions, language, and behaviour are coherent and harmonious.

Step 2: Action

Actions within the organization should reflect the mindset and be based on a set of guiding principles. They should be a commitment to learning over time, formulated in a "learning mode," and involve a constant process of doing, reflecting, and consulting. It is crucial to think through actions carefully, considering their long-term effects and alignment with the original vision. There should also be space for spontaneous acts of kindness, allowing room for human connection.

Step 3: Reflection and Learning

Learning through reflection is a means of focusing the mind and gaining wisdom from experience, applicable in both personal and commercial spheres. Setting aside time for reflection, learning from data and reports, and measuring outcomes beyond just financial metrics can significantly alter the course of a business for the better. Regular meetings for progress checks, idea sharing, and support rallying are vital. Reflective thinking enhances decision-making, productivity, and overall impact, providing a firm foundation for growth.

METHOD APPLIED

In my role as a surgeon, I've observed the healthcare industry's culture and recognized its divergence from my personal beliefs. Yet, I've leveraged my unique approach to positively influence our internal teams. My primary mindset revolves around service, compassion, and accompaniment, especially when dealing with anxious parents awaiting their child's diagnosis. To alleviate this stress, I implemented a policy with my staff to see new patients with a possible diagnosis of a tumor within 24 hours, emphasizing swift, compassionate care.

Furthermore, I instructed our frontline team to prioritize the human connection. Their role wasn't just to answer calls but to empathize and connect. Navigating the healthcare landscape is already complicated and frustrating enough patients and their families, so focusing on connecting and accompaniment is something that we can do with minimal effort and cost. By prioritizing the human connection, we started to focus on emphasizing strong interpersonal skills in our hiring process over previous healthcare experience. I also empowered my team with the autonomy to act humanely, even providing them with a credit card to express compassion, such as sending condolences. However, I also ensured they had the resources they needed, encouraging them to signal when additional staff was required.

This strategy, rooted in my mindset, began reshaping our team's behaviour, enhancing our organization's effectiveness, and solidifying our reputation as a trusted healthcare provider.

Questions to ask in team reflections:

1. How closely do our organizational values align with our day-to-day actions and decision-making processes?
2. Are we consistently reflecting our internal values in our external interactions and services?
3. How can we prioritize the human connection in our organization, especially in customer interactions and internal team dynamics?

THE TRANSFORMATION

By applying the above methodology, what kind of changes can you likely observe?

Overtime, if you have not employed a comparable method, a notable transformation that could emerge is the gradual and complete involvement of individuals. Traditional management often funnels ideas, restricting creativity and innovation. However, when you foster a culture where individuals dare to question and bring their full curiosity to the table, you unlock a reservoir of potential. This not only enhances efficiency but also nurtures the human spirit, preventing employees from becoming mere drones and echo chambers for backbiting. By creating open spaces, as previously mentioned, you offer employees opportunities to innovate without boundaries, especially in regulated environments like healthcare. Such unrestricted zones balance the inherent human need for creativity against the confines of their daily tasks. In essence, this approach ensures that while some structures guide the organization, there's ample room for innovation, ensuring a harmonious blend of structure and spontaneity. Most importantly, by enabling your organization to embark on a journey focused on both individuals and collective capacity building, you are fostering resilience and organizational adaptability that will endure for decades.

This transformation is not only crucial on the level of business survival but also has profound ramifications for society. Let me share with you a personal story to illustrate my point: My grandmother, a 92-year-old woman with longstanding, well controlled congestive heart failure, was hospitalized after a fall. At home, she was on a salt-restricted diet and weighed herself daily monitoring her fluid levels. In the hospital, as she didn't speak English well, the staff would order her meals. One day, she was served a salt-rich meal which included meatloaf, French fries and a coke. In a country in which 75% of adults 60 years old and over have a hypertension requiring a salt restricted diet, having a 92 year old on a "normal diet" is beyond rare. Naturally, I inquired and the nurses simply stated she wasn't on a restricted diet. This lack of basic judgment and questioning enabled a clerical error in the electronic medical record to lead to her untimely death. Such oversights stem from a system where individuals, even educated ones, cease to question what is obvious, and to think independently. When we prioritize top-down approaches and stringent rules, we stifle the human spirit of inquiry and curiosity, turning professionals into mere drones. Like the hospital incident, the absence of questioning can lead to grave errors and no amount of rules can anticipate every challenge.

I firmly believe that every successful organization, whether a hospital or a Fortune 500 company, must foster a culture of curiosity and creativity. Without deliberate safeguarding and support, as these organizations expand, this essence can fade, leading the organization to lose its vitality and drift into death. Thus, it's imperative to preserve the innate curiosity we all possess. As illustrated, this transformation can not only help businesses survive but in some cases can actually save lives.

TAKE HOME ADVICE

Embarking on this transformative journey, it's essential to understand the essence of community within an organization. Here are two pivotal pieces of advice to ensure success:

1) Regular Reflection: Initiate a monthly reflection meeting with your teams. The goal is use it for practical reverse engineering. In your first meetings delve into questions like:

- How do we define our community within the organization and what characteristics or attributes distinguish us?
- How do we envision our organization functioning as a community, and what structures or practices can we implement to align with this vision?
- What values and virtues do we want to embody?
- How can our product or service positively impact society and our stakeholders? What do we need to embody as a team to achieve this coherently?

- How does our product or service serve humanity beyond its functional purpose, and what additional value or impact does it bring to society?

Again the goal is to have the end in mind, no matter how hard it may seem. Then act towards that goal, ensuring that you create a culture in which time is allocated for reflection and discussion, which ultimately enables alignment around a shared vision.

2) Challenge the Status Quo: In the journey towards organizational excellence, its critical to recognize the delicate balance between fostering a vibrant and dynamic community versus merely following current trends and expectations.

- **Differentiate Community from Comfort:** It's essential to distinguish between building a genuine community within the organization and merely providing a comfortable workspace. True community involves deeper connections and shared goals.
- **Embrace Challenges as Opportunities:** While comfort is desirable, the reality is that all meaningful work will eventually face tests and challenges. View tests and challenges not as obstacles but as opportunities for significant growth and reasons for celebration. This mindset shift can transform the approach to problem-solving and innovation.
- **Foster Collaborative Approaches:** Encourage a collaborative environment where even the most demanding tasks can be approached with joy and fulfilment. Collaboration enhances team spirit and leads to more effective solutions.

- **Build Unity Through Action:** Leaders should focus on building unity of thought and then through collective action, and should guard against creating an overly sensitive environment. Unity fosters a strong team dynamic that can withstand challenges.
- **Preserve the Human Spirit of Questioning:** Maintaining a culture of curiosity and creativity is crucial for organizational vitality. Encourage team member to question, explore and innovate to prevent stagnation.

As I conclude this chapter, its essential to reiterate the importance of a posture of learning as an organization which involves making mistakes. Rage against the natural temptation of creating an environment of celebration in which mistakes are hidden, even worse, not even seen because of egos.

ABOUT THE AUTHOR

Dr. Salim Afshar is a Harvard-trained surgeon and healthcare technologist with a background in advancing global health systems through innovation and technology. As Chief Medical Officer at Reveal HealthTech, he merges clinical expertise and healthcare systems knowledge with a profound grasp of engineering to aid healthcare entities in adopting and integrating technology effectively. He is an active member of the United Nations Innovation Exchange and provides guidance to multiple companies as an advisor and board member. In his surgical career, he performed nearly 6,000 operations, specializing in rare pediatric head and neck conditions, and has developed a novel use of AI within his specialty. Dr. Afshar is also an author, with numerous academic and non-academic articles addressing AI's impact on global health, the democratization of healthcare, and the nexus of healthcare with technology, particularly in cancer care. He is deeply committed to enhancing healthcare by integrating clinical insights into software development and championing technology solutions that are both innovative and practical.

Vision and Imagination: How to Create a Better Kind of Organization

Roy Steiner

—

Senior Vice President, The Rockefeller Foundation

"Special regard must
be paid to agriculture.
Unquestionably
it precedes...
peace, education,
universal language."

The Writings
of Bahá'u'lláh

I believe the right words, said at the right time, can set us on a path for life.

My journey to working in regenerative agriculture began as a child, when my mother showed me the quotation above from the Writings of the Bahá'í Faith – a religion that teaches the unity of all people. She recognised that, aged 12, I loved plants and she encouraged me to pursue my interests. One magical day she gave me a plot of land and said: "You can grow whatever you want."

It was only a small garden plot, but I loved the miracle of planting seeds and watching them blossom and ripen into foods we can eat and share with others. At that transformative moment, agriculture came into my life – and it never left.

Today, I run the Food Initiative at the Rockefeller Foundation, leading long-term philanthropic projects to develop more nourishing, regenerative and equitable food systems across the world. Having spent decades in this field, my job is to find out how we can help transform the world's food production systems, which are currently failing both people and the planet.

What we are eating is – quite literally – killing us. Diet is the number-one risk for early mortality globally, and how we are growing our food is destroying the planet. Our food production systems contribute more than 30 per cent of global greenhouse gas emissions, and consume over 70% of our freshwater resources.

Over the years, I have funded and run research programs that aim to either improve dietary quality or create a regenerative food system. Our work is global, but we focus on Africa and the United States. The challenge for our planet is huge:

- 811 million people are severely undernourished
- Three billion people do not have access to healthy diets
- 90 million children under five are dangerously underweight
- 34 per cent of greenhouse gas emissions come from food systems

IMAGINING A NEW FUTURE, AND TRYING TO MAKE IT POSSIBLE

If you review the hundreds of books and movies that describe the future, the visions they show are almost entirely dark and dystopian. Take the films *Mad Max* and *Hunger Games*, for instance: these are dark and dangerous worlds ruled by violence and savagery.

Humanity is great at describing the future we don't want. We dedicate our best minds and millions of dollars of Hollywood investment to creating these terrible, apocalyptic scenarios. But we invest little time and energy into describing worlds we actually want, and how to make them possible.

Why is this? One reason is that it is far easier to tell stories that reinforce negativity, rather than championing positive forces in our society. It is also hard to tell 'good news' stories that don't sound fake.

Humans are traditionally hardwired to be prepared that things will go wrong, rather than believing in what is possible.

In essence, one of the major problems we have is a lack of hope, and I think it's because we have a lack of positive models to inspire us. When we are presented with so many examples of things going wrong, we don't pay attention to the things that are going right.

But what if we switched this around? What if we started spending 98% of our time imagining and describing a positive future, and only 2% of our time and energy talking about all the problems in the world? Positive visualization leads to manifestation of positive change – and if we all follow this process, imagine what a better reality we could create.

We could start by describing worlds where we have found a solution to climate change, there is true equality, human well being is at the centre of every decision, and societies are governed by justice and fairness. Once crime and corruption are eradicated, the resources we spend tackling problems in our society could be redeployed to make everyone wealthier.

We can start imagining a better future, by asking ourselves simple questions such as.

- If we made all the right decisions, what kind of world could we create?
- What are the most important steps to create this world?
- What would it look like if...?

THE ROCKEFELLER FOUNDATION VISION PRIZE

To help visualize and develop more regenerative systems, the Rockefeller Foundation launched a Vision Prize to organizations from around the world. More than 1,300 groups shared their collective visions of the local foods systems they wanted – food systems that were nutritious, economically equitable, supportive of community and culture and environmentally sustainable.

The responses we received were exciting and inspiring. It's hard to encourage people to stretch their minds more than a year, or five years, into the future. But once you start looking forward ten, 20, or even 50 years, the possibilities are endless and the process is incredibly freeing.

Expanding our historical perspectives is critical, so we remember how much progress can be made in a relatively short time. For instance, 100 years ago women in the US had only recently won the right to vote after years of struggle, and ending racial segregation was still a dream – it would not be outlawed until the Civil Rights Act in 1964.

From the thousands of entries for the Foundation's Vision Prize, we chose ten overall prize-winners from every corner of the world.

Among them there was a compelling idea for the Rosebud Reservation Sioux Tribe in South Dakota, currently the third-poorest state in the US. It imagined a food system where buffalo had been brought back into the life of the Sioux community on the Wolakota Buffalo Range: an area of native grassland covering almost 28,000 acres.

The project team released 100 buffalos from nearby national parks into this territory in 2020. Today, the herd is helping promote ecological restoration, economic development, food security and public education within the Sioux reservation.

In India, the Aruku coffee-growing community completely changed the economics of the food production system so the farmer comes first, and therefore receives sufficient profits to live well. The entire systems is designed to prioritize farmers rather than distant coffee traders who used to capture most of the profits.

This vision was fully aligned with the Writings of the Bahá'í Faith which emphasizes the need to put "farmers first".

The Rockefeller Foundation's Vision Prize helped communities and organizations trigger their imagination to visualize a better future for the entire world, because if we can envision it, we can believe it. And it is only if we believe in it that we will build it.

HOW CAN WE CREATE A VISIONARY ORGANISATION?

The Bahá'í Writings state that peace is not only possible, but inevitable. However, whether we choose it through an act of consultative will or unimaginable pain and suffering, is the choice we all have before us.

Since we must start building this better world somewhere, why not start by changing how we work? It's how we spend the majority of our waking hours and the driver of global economies. I believe that ethical businesses can help build the future if they follow the steps for creating a visionary and imaginative organisation outlined here.

1. Establish your principles

One interesting thing I learned about visions is that you must start from a set of principle. If you don't start with principles if becomes more difficult to resolve disagreements, and people start focusing on the problems and not on the solutions. If you haven't established a set of principles at the beginning, you can't come back to them at a later stage to resolve the conflict.

2. Make a clear plan to achieve your goals

We have already established that to build the future we must be visionary and imaginative. Those are the core skills, but a vision without a plan is simply wishful thinking. Furthermore, translating this vision into action cannot happen without a learning process – and as part of that, we must learn to accept failure. Acknowledging failure means accepting that learning means making mistakes, evolving, trying new paths to achieve the best result.

We know there must be an accountability for what we do. But if everybody knows they have their own personal development program, this gives them a goal. Their goal becomes your goal, and everybody gains. This is how you create a culture of learning, and a culture of trust.

3. Evaluate progress along the way

I firmly believe in the power of honest feedback systems that show whether your projects and plans are effective. The best organizations regularly carry out quick surveys to check in with their customers or employees. This helps them calibrate their plans and adapt their corporate thinking. Poor performing organizations do the same surveys, but they don't listen to them. If you don't set up systematic feedback, chances are you will waste time on things that don't matter.

CHALLENGING QUESTIONS

- Can you imagine and visualize the future 20 years from now?
- Now visualize the future you would like for your children in 20 years' time. Is it the same?
- What are your principles for your vision? Do they also influence your attitude at work, with your team or employees?
- Can you learn from your mistakes and adapt your plans if things go wrong?
- Do you accept feedback as part of your learning process?

ABOUT THE AUTHOR

Roy Steiner is the Managing Director of the Food Initiative at The Rockefeller Foundation. He is committed to developing a food system that is regenerative, nourishing and equitable.

How to Nourish Your Inner Leader

Jaleh Zandieh

—

Global Leadership Consultant for Service Driven Leaders & Their Teams to Create a Culture of Empowerment & Inclusion

*"Make sure everybody
in the company
has great opportunities,
has a meaningful impact
and is contributing
to the good of society."*

Larry Page,
CEO, Google

WHY SHOULD ETHICAL BUSINESSES BUILD THE FUTURE?

HOW SHOULD ETHICAL BUSINESSES BUILD THE FUTURE?

In my 21 years of research and working with over 6,500 industry leaders from 51 countries I've seen consistent proof that a growing model of culture-building is not only possible, but is also emerging and developing stronger roots. This model uplifts the quality of life, health, happiness, and success of all the people involved.

How can this become the New Normal? I've looked at multiple factors over the last two decades and the data is consistent – across cultures, economies, and industries:

The success of an environment, company, and organization improves significantly when certain capacities are invested in and cultivated to the point of deep trust, excellence, and resilience. One of the most important sources of energy for this transformation is a central value and priority on service – both to the individual and to the collective.

There is a great variety of challenges and historical patterns of division, prejudice, and injustice that causes many communities to be overlooked, undervalued, and underserved. Lacking opportunities and access to quality health, education, and other fundamental needs diminishes what human beings are experiencing throughout the world.

Ethical leaders help create and innovate new opportunities for people and communities to uplevel their health, progress, and capacity to help others.

Ethical businesses who strive to serve all stakeholders in their ecosystem can become champions of policies that improve the quality of life for the leadership, the teams, the employees, the customers, the clients, the market, the economy, the environment, and the industries that they impact.

These types of companies can continue to be a symbol of hope, inspiration, and a catalyst for other leaders to make these same choices:

A) Having a clear vision that stands for honesty, respect, dignity, justice, creativity, trust, cooperation, community, generosity, accountability, and humanity.

B) Honoring the core values in decision-making that are designed to amplify the potential, well-being, and talents of each person in the organization.

C) Building a brand voice that expresses the vision and values in practical ways.

Business leaders who choose to be ethical each day are improving the lives of people – directly and indirectly – by demonstrating what's possible, that a higher standard of conduct exists, that success is possible without harming others, being dedicated to learning how to make each day better than yesterday based on our choices today.

No matter the size or location of the company, team, or organization – these principles remained consistent. My research suggests that ethical business practices yield greater rewards in many areas: financially, socially, morally, legally, creatively, and many others.

Over the course of my career, thousands of service-driven industry leaders communicated that it's their moral imperative and duty to use their power, resources, and network to do good in the world. They expressed that this responsibility was not imposed by others, but that they found tremendous satisfaction and fulfillment in prioritizing ethical standards in their organizations. They felt appreciation for the fact that their success could open doors of opportunities and uplift people and communities.

Doing their work ethically and with a central theme on service was not a drain on their time or energy, but rather it was a way to feel that they were using their time and energy well. They felt joy in seeing the ripples of impact of their work, teams, and projects.

Here are some examples of what successful, service-driven leaders sound like:

"Why not proactively put processes, plans, preparations in place to help my team thrive?"

"What better reason to get out of bed in the morning than to see how my day can be used well to help others succeed?"

"My premeditated desire is to infuse more good into the world so there is less struggle, stress, suffering."

"When my company does well, I can't wait to share bonus checks with my staff – since they're the ones who worked hard to help the business succeed."

"My parents weren't proud of my when I made my first million dollars. They were proud of me when I gave my first million away to help a children's hospital in my hometown."

"Success means I get to lift more people up so that their lives and their families improve."

"Looking out for others is what makes me happy at the end of the day. That's how I know that it was a productive day."

"If my team feels encouraged by my actions, then I'm doing my job as the leader."

"My first responsibility is to create an environment that keeps them firmly in their power... so they help each other instead of trying to steal power or peace from anyone else. Truly powerful people don't want to engage in destructive patterns that cause mistrust or pain for other people, such as belittling or bullying. There's no place for that in our company."

Ethical business choose to create environments where people feel safe to work and contribute their talents or expertise, as well as foster healthy communication and cooperation between people so they can all do their best work. Higher retention and work satisfaction consistently occur when people feel appreciated, enjoy bonds of friendship and respectful conversations, and feel invested in. Organizations that prioritize these elements in their culture experience these significant metrics for success.

Ethical business will continue to be a force that changes the tides of historical patterns and foster healthier, more united and productive companies, communities, cultures, and society.

A focal point of my research and consulting with service-driven businesses and organziations has been on how to create a thriving culture that nurtures the best and brightest contributions of the entire team.

A thriving, united team can lead to higher satisfaction, retention, productivity, lasting client relationships, brand loyalty, respect, financial scalability, and greater peace of mind for the owners.

Five consistent patterns and trends in successful, ethical leadership that I've seen throughout my career and experience is that they:

A) Train & Retain Leadership Qualities That Serve & Embody the Values of the Business

B) Develop and Invest in a Team That Trusts Themselves & Each Other

C) Have a Quality Reputation That Attracts Collaborations & Opportunities

D) Support a Thriving Culture That Attracts Best & Brightest Experts

E) Believe That Success is Not Meant to Be Lonely so They Create a Powerful Community of fellow service-driven, ethical leaders in their network and friendship circles.

Ethical business prioritize culture-building with the pillar and practical commitment to service, advancing their respect and reputation in their industry. This attracts and retains the best and brightest talented experts and employees. These reciprocally beneficial elements in the environment cultivate a greater motivation and desire for excellence.

The values of service and encouragement help members of the team feel a sense of loyalty, ownership, and responsibility to deliver their best to clients, customers, employees, managers, collaborators, and all other stakeholders.

Ethical values being center stage attracts best and brightest, and once they're part of the team they want to be part of the progress, success, and expansion of the organization.

These business leaders attract like-minded, trained professionals with shared values that form a united vision and roles to play. Service-driven professionals want to be affiliated with high caliber companies and organizations who have a noteworthy reputation for being trustworthy, respected industry leaders. Doing great actions and having policies that increase the quality of life for people truly stands out and gives reasons as why ethical policies are a trend for companies who want to be resilient and successful through any type of challenge.

Having an ethical standard allows companies to attract greater loyalty, praise, and opportunities from raving fan customers and clients. It has been seen to be an efficient way to expand as brand recognition and strong collaborations with other ethical businesses and titans of industry – raising the level of visibility and respect.

Ethical businesses cultivate greater trust and integrity which leads to higher levels of respect, retention, recognition, and reputation. Each of these can yield greater financial, social, economic, and philanthropic impact.

CHALLENGING QUESTIONS

- What are your tips – practical steps – useful actions that you would share with readers eager to be "ethical people building the future"?
- Learn, develop and understand your unique Leadership Style because this is a powerful way to achieve fulfilling success for yourself AND impact others by supporting their success.
- Invest in the Leadership potential, capacities, and understanding you and your team's Leadership Style because this is a powerful, effective way to achieve fulfilling success for yourself AND others as you co-create a thriving culture.
- Whatever stage of leadership you're currently in, increase your capacity and creativity to do acts of service for others that are also joyful for you because it creates a powerful ripple effect that supports everyone's success.

ABOUT THE AUTHOR

Her system helps entrepreneurs and business leaders enrich and uplevel the leadership capacities of them and their teams so that they can create a legacy of community and inclusion. This leads to greater impact and success that's nourished by the 9 diverse elements of their Leadership Styles.

Jaleh's foundational Philosophy: "Success requires dedicated self-mastery. Self-mastery requires nourishment of many capacities. Diversity is an essential element that nourishes our talents & gifts."

"Nourished by Diversity" is her newest book.

When Jaleh's not creating customized experiences for innovative leaders around the world, she's filling her passport with stamps to discover hidden gems, savoring exotic teas, and loves dancing to local music with her hubby in Portugal.

Faith in Business

Steve Sarowitz

—

Founder of Paylocity
CEO of Blue Marble — Director of Payescape
Co-Chairman at Wayfarer Studios
Board of NCAT

"So powerful is the light
of unity that
it can illuminate
the whole earth."

'Abdu'l-Bahá,
The Promulgation
of Universal Peace

LONG-TERM PHILANTHROPY VERSUS BAND-AID PHILANTHROPY

Philanthropy is helping the world; giving away money in the hope of making the world a better place.

But all too often it's handled as *band-aid philanthropy*. For example, let's take homeless people. Instead of trying to figure out why they're homeless, we offer them housing. This isn't a *bad* thing, but it won't solve the problem. For a long-term solution, we must understand what's causing their homelessness. Similarly, if we really want to feed the hungry, we must figure out why they're hungry. What causes the inequity?

Band-aid philanthropy doesn't go to the root of the problem. In the long run, you're not making the world a better place, because the poor remain poor and still need to be fed. A better solution is a long-term vision that asks: **What's the cause of this?** Can we get at the root cause? Can we make a systemic change that will prevent the problem in the first place? It is like preventative health, and this is the type of philanthropy I prefer to focus on.

A friend of mine helped a couple of homeless people get a home. But he didn't realize that the root cause of their homelessness wasn't their material inability to afford a house. Giving them housing didn't actually solve the problem – it made it worse, because the root cause of their homelessness went much deeper. They were drug addicts and because he got them a house, they had more money, which they used for more drugs. One of them was hospitalized in a very short time and almost died; the other also suffered.

People get hooked on drugs and alcohol because they have a hole in their heart. If you want to take them one level further, they must confront themselves with their spiritual problem. Almost every problem in the world is spiritual, not material. We are primarily spiritual beings.

My favorite question (especially for young people) is:
What have you done to feed your soul today?

If you've done nothing, you'll feed it with something, like drugs or alcohol.

Philanthropy means financing activities to make the world a better place.

Effective philanthropy finds the root of the problem and tries to solve it.

HOW CAN FAITH HELP THE BUSINESS WORLD?

Teenagers today in the United States (and elsewhere) have massive issues with depression, mental illness, drugs, and alcohol.

I was one of the judges at a contest held at the University of Chicago, where entrepreneurs present their projects to a group of investors, and they have to decide who's worth the investment. One business said they were there to help kids with mental illness. I asked if faith played a role in their work. The woman presenting the project said they allowed people to talk about their faith, but they were doing pure group counseling. In other words, they didn't recognize that the lack of faith today is a major issue. They acknowledged it existed, but it wasn't part of their solution. I said to the other judges that this approach was like looking at a table of starving people and saying food wasn't an option. We're all spiritually starving. This goes not just for these kids but for businesses as well.

But there are a few things we need to consider if we want faith to become an important part of our businesses.

The effects of spiritual starvation on business

Managing human resources becomes really hard, because people are upset, depressed, and angry.

I've been a Baha'i for eight years, and when I entered the Faith I'd tell people the world was disintegrating, most people would look at me like I was crazy. Today, just eight years later, almost everybody readily agrees with me when I talk about the world's disintegration.

When I follow up with, "Well, what are we going to do about it?" the conversation gets quieter.

There's a dual process of disintegration and integration. Philanthropy must be part of that integration, and the remaking of philanthropy as an essentially spiritual enterprise is where my interest lies.

I have helped fund two foundations – the Julian Grace Foundation, which I started with my wife, and Wayfarer Foundation, my personal Baha'i-inspired foundation. On the board we have three Baha'is (including myself). The foundation is relatively young, almost two and a half years old. In the first year, we gave away $4 million. Last year, we gave away a little over $9 million, and this year it will be $19 million. The goal is to eventually reach between $50 to $100 million a year. We're rapidly ramping up our giving.

We ask every granting partner about their spiritual purpose, and some of them look at us funny. But many are grateful we ask that question. It's an essential part of what we're doing. We work with communities and focus on who has the voice in the room.

It's important to address the spiritual and the practical together. Many foundations and philanthropists focus solely on material solutions and miss the spiritual dimension. They lack the understanding of the need for spiritual solutions if we truly want to make a difference.

It's hard to unify people without faith

When I'm running a business, faith is really important. While I don't mind if someone is not religious, I won't hire an employee who's actively anti religion. First, they probably wouldn't want me as a boss because I'm religious. Second, it would be very hard for me to inspire them, and we'll probably have a problem because typically if you're anti religion, you're also very likely skeptical of religious people.

There's no reason for you to do what's right or wrong and there's no moral basis for your actions. If you work in a no-faith environment, there's no morality, because the keeper of morality is religion. Not many people are willing to admit that. For example, why wouldn't you steal if you had no belief? Nothing will stop you from doing it. This is the reason that societies like Russia that have done away with religion often have problems with corruption.

UNITY, THE KEY FACTOR TOWARD EFFECTIVE DIVERSITY

I apply the principle of unity in everything I do. Today, one of the biggest issues in business is diversity. But why are we looking for diversity? To check a box? If that's the case, you're going about diversity in the wrong way.

Instead of forcing diversity, why not embrace it?

If you want to promote diversity, it should be because you want to do it, not because you're forced to. If you're just doing it because someone made you, you won't have any passion for it. Anything done without passion isn't done well. Nowadays, companies must be diverse, but instead of being forced, why not embrace it?

True faith teaches us to embrace diversity; my faith teaches us that we're one human family. I passionately want to promote diversity, not because I'm forced to, not because someone is making me do this, but because I passionately believe everyone is equal and deserves every opportunity. I'm genuinely happy to give opportunities to people who've been denied them, like people of color and women. When you have joy in what you do, everything turns out better.

We're entering an age in which the aspects of humanity where women have been traditionally stronger have become necessary: compassion, unity, cooperation, and peace. For centuries, the world has been male-dominated. If you go back a couple of hundred years, women were virtually slaves in every country in the world. But we're coming out of this and facing rapid change.

I recently spoke to a group of women who were campaigning to ban assault weapons in the United States after a mass shooting in my city. They're working very hard, and a group of men doing this wouldn't have had the same impact. Women bring a different perspective and approach to these issues. They have a lot to say, but unfortunately, we aren't listening to them yet. Investing in women, internally and externally, is one of my goals. As women rise and have their voices heard, things will change for the better for all of us.

It would be an amazing world if women were given their full voice and agency, and if they were leading side by side with men.

Many years ago, long before most people started talking about diversity, I founded a company called Paylocity – a company providing cloudcloud-based payroll and human capital management software. We hired the best people we could. But we always hired white men for upper management. We had one woman who was also white. This wasn't because we were prejudiced; we never set out to avoid hiring black people. It was because our networks and the people who had the experience and opportunities were primarily white men. Society was geared towards white men.

Paylocity and many other companies have changed. Our hires have diversified. Both employees and the board have become more diverse. However, trying to become diverse is not always an easy task.

At one point, the CEO and I had called a search firm for hiring new board members. When they asked what I wanted for the board, what changes I wanted, I told them diversity was my number one objective. But despite this, they brought us all white male candidates.

I was proud of the CEO, because he sent them back and said, "Excuse me, we told you diversity was important. Go back to the drawing board. There's nothing wrong with these candidates. It is not that they aren't qualified, but we told you diversity was important."

Sometimes you must be determined in fighting for your cause. We told them to look harder. And they did. They eventually found us wonderful candidates who were diverse.

The benefits and impact of diversity on business

Paylocity has become the fastest growing publicly held payroll and HR provider in the world over the last year. You can't argue with success. We were successful before we applied the principle of diversity, but we're even more successful now.

Certain people in high-level positions are really contributing toward that success; some people we brought in are doing an absolutely great job. They enjoy their work and we've definitely benefited from that. When you make decisions, you want differing points of view. You want different opinions, because out of the clash of conflicting ideas comes the spark of truth according to the Baha'ì Faith's concept of consultation. With a single point of view, you're going to miss things. When you bring in diversity, you get different viewpoints and it becomes a richer, fuller experience for everyone involved.

PARTNERING WITH PEOPLE SHARING THE SAME VISION AND VALUES TO FOSTER UNITY AND PROFIT

My experience with Justin Baldoni and Jamey Heath at the Wayfarer Production Company demonstrates my point of view.

Our company wants to upend the traditional Hollywood studio model by putting equity and social justice at the forefront, and it specializes in producing contents addressing social issues.

We have an incredibly kind and loving relationship which makes everything so much better. During one of our shoots there was a strike going on and we lost a few days. Each lost day cost us $300,000. The pressure was very high because it was a very high-profile movie shoot.

I said to my partners we were in a foxhole, referencing a saying from World War One: “There are no atheists in a foxhole”.

All three of us are passionate Bahá’ís. I told them, “There’s no one else I’d want to be in a foxhole with. I’d rather lose with you guys than anyone else”. I love them that much. To have partners who love you and to love your partners and to enjoy going to work is a blessing and a key to true success.

I read about a very successful investment company where the two partners just couldn’t get along. It had got to the point where it was affecting the financial success of the firm, as well as of its employees. Our employees are positively affected by our approach and, most importantly, we’re positively influenced by them. All three of us share our Faith’s vision for making the world a better place, treating people with respect, and making the oneness of the human family.

It’s very important that partners share the same vision. This creates a strong bond, a unity. Like the Christian Bible says, a divided house can’t stand.

TIPS FOR A NEW BUSINESS

Have a sense of purpose: the ultimate purpose in life is to be a better human being

We're not here on Earth just to make the most money or have the most power. We're here to make the world a better place. If we're serious about every step we take, it will make us much happier and more productive. Even if you don't end up being the richest person, you'll be happier, more fulfilled, and much nicer. That's the most important thing.

A friend of mine is an atheist. He has a very successful business, but he struggles with purpose. I'd love to help him, but I can't; I can't force my faith on him. His business is great, and he's a good man, but he'd be happier if he had faith. He's built a very successful business, but he isn't sure why. Even financially, he isn't sure what to do. He's bought things but that hasn't brought him happiness. In contrast, I'm very, very happy. I'm wealthy too, but you need a sense of purpose to feel fulfilled. What is the sense of being rich if you don't have a purpose?

Never sacrifice your morality

Fatollah Ferdowsi is one of my idols and my goal is to be like him. He was killed in Iran for his Baha'I Faith. His story was wonderfully told by his son Farsheed in his book Under the Staircase.

When Fatollah shook your hand, you didn't need a contract. Once you shook his hand, the deal was done. Of course, he did use contracts, but he was so well respected that he didn't need them. Probably the best story in the book is about when he did business with a Muslim vendor. Fatollah treated everyone with respect, regardless of their faith. This Muslim man had borrowed too much money and was going to have to declare bankruptcy. In Iran, going bankrupt meant you were out of business for life.

Even though they weren't close friends, Fatollah decided to help him and renegotiated with the banks. Since he was so respected, the banks agreed to give this man a second chance. However, a year later the Iranian revolution broke out and Fatollah saw the man in a crowd of people loudly denouncing the Baha'ì people. Fatollah was distraught; he felt like a Jew being denounced by a Nazi in the time of Hitler.

Shortly after, the man was involved in a terrible car accident and Fatollah visited him in the hospital. That is a man of tremendous integrity and forgiveness. I want to be known as that man. When I recognized my faith, I declared it in front of a portrait of ninety-nine martyrs who'd been killed in Iran. Fatollah was at the center of that picture.

CHALLENGING QUESTIONS

- Has faith ever been a decisive factor in your business decisions?
- Do you encourage diversity in your company?
- What is your purpose in life and in your business?
- Did you ever sacrifice morality for business profit? (If yes, how did you feel afterward?)

ABOUT THE AUTHOR

Steve Sarowitz is founder and Chairman of Paylocity, a leading US provider of payroll and HR solutions. In addition, Steve serves as Director of Payescape, a United Kingdom payroll provider. He's also an international philanthropist with an interest in promoting unity, supporting universal education and advocating for the elimination of racism, sexism, nationalism, and religious prejudice. His family foundation supports over fifty worthy causes worldwide, including programs helping orphans, foster children, refugees, and many other people in need. Steve is an avid runner, a member of the Chicago Area Runners Association Hall of Fame and a three-time winner of the MSE Division of the Chicago Chase Corporate Challenge. He's also the co-Chairman of Wayfarer Studios and was Executive Producer for the award-winning documentary Maya Angelou: And Still I Rise. *Steve is also the producer of The Gate, a groundbreaking documentary about the founding of the Baha'i Faith.*

Sovaida Ma'ani

How to Identify Your Mission in Life and Use It to Uplift Your Workplace: Harnessing the Power of Distinctive Capabilities.

Sovaida Ma'ani

—

Co-Owner at Unleash Your Coaching

"What is the use of living,
if it be not to strive for
noble causes and to make
this muddled world
a better place for those
who will live in it after
we are gone?"

Winston Churchill

WHY SHOULD WE ENSURE THAT ETHICAL BUSINESS BUILDS THE FUTURE?

The simple answer is because doing so enables us to achieve two key purposes in life: acquiring those virtues of character that enable us to become the best and highest version of ourselves; and living life in service to others while working in concert and harmony with each other towards the unified goal of making this world a better place.

Imagine a **crucible**, a container designed to endure intense heat, where raw materials are melted, reshaped and transformed into tools that can be used in bettering the human condition. Now consider that the world of business is akin to such a forge, namely, a transformative space in which the iron of our character is shaped and molded, often with a fair degree of pain. It is here, among the challenges and opportunities of our work life that our character – just like iron – is repeatedly tested, refined, and ultimately defined.

We come to see, therefore, that business is not merely a realm of transactions and profits; it is a **theater of learning, growth, and transformation**. It offers us a unique platform to set aside our ego (or at least round off its rough edges) and exclusive focus on self-interest, to collaborate on shared goals, and elevate our collective aspirations.

For many, the tumultuous landscape of business may seem an unlikely place to seek enlightenment or personal growth. Yet, it is precisely in this environment that we discover and actualize our true potential. Business, when approached with integrity and vision, becomes more than just a material enterprise. It becomes transformed into a mission, a quest to bring value that transcends monetary measurement, and a conduit for fulfilling our deepest purpose in life.

Redefining success: from profit to value

Over the years, I've had the privilege of engaging with CEOs of many successful companies in the context of my coaching activities. In my interactions with them, a recurring theme has emerged: the essence of business isn't just wealth accumulation. It's about **creating and giving value**. Money, while essential, is not, in itself sufficient. On one hand, it is but a byproduct of this value-driven mission, on the other it represents an exchange of energy. Many who are at the pinnacle of their industries recognize this, understanding that genuine success is not measured in dollars but in the positive contribution they make to the betterment of people's lives.

As we navigate the challenges of our times, ethical businesses stand out as beacons of hope. **They are uniquely positioned to bake value into the building-blocks of our society**. They remind us that, even in the face of adversity, we possess the power to shape the world we envision – a world where peace and prosperity flourish – by taking responsibility for our choices. That's why ethical businesses have the potential of being the **architects of a more equitable and peaceful future for humanity**.

THE FORMULA FOR AN ETHICAL BUSINESS: ONENESS + JUSTICE + LOVE

Over the past two decades, my work has spanned two distinct spheres: firstly, contribution to the transformation of global governance by proposing principled solutions to seemingly intractable global challenges. My overarching goal has been to help our human family take the next step in its collective growth towards maturity. Secondly, coaching individuals to transform their lives and steadily actualize their innate potential. Through these experiences, I've discerned a foundational truth: before making decisions at any level of society, be it tackling global challenges like the war in Ukraine, or resolving personal dilemmas like whether to continue one's career or stay home and parent, it's imperative to first **identify the underlying principles and then apply them to addressing the question at hand**. Similarly, before establishing any institution, including a business, we must pinpoint its guiding principles.

Just as in mathematics, identifying and mastering first **principles allows us to derive formulas to solve problems**, so, too, in life and business, starting from first principles is essential. They should be intricately woven into the very fabric of any organization and into every process. My twenty-five-year journey has taught me that identifying, agreeing upon, and applying three particular principles can yield elegant and coherent solutions to complex issues:

Oneness

emphasizes the interconnectedness and interdependence of all individuals (and nations). In the context of a business, every member of the organization, regardless of their role, contributes unique and crucial value. This principle challenges the traditional hierarchical structures where decisions are top-down. Instead, it values the inherent worth of each person and creates an inclusive and collaborative environment where diverse talents and perspectives are harnessed for a greater good, while fostering individual and collective growth.

Justice

is not just about fairness in decision-making but also about ensuring that every individual (and nation, in the context of global governance) has the opportunity to realize their potential. It's about creating a level playing field where decisions are made transparently and every voice is valued, giving people an equal chance to contribute and grow.

Love

is not necessarily about feelings, it's about learning to appreciate and truly value ourselves and others. It's recognizing and respecting the unique contributions each individual brings to the table, creating deeper bonds of solidarity and common purpose inside an organization.

Oneness, justice and love are not isolated principles but are deeply interconnected. When combined, they create a harmonious framework for ethical decision-making and action and provide a roadmap to create the right conditions for ethical organizations to flourish.

How do these principles help business transformation?

In today's world, we witness the failure of various systems, from politics to business. Despite having achieved success, status, and wealth, many of us still find ourselves in toxic environments, feeling unfulfilled and miserable. How might things change if we infused these three principles into our organizations and daily lives?

A re-definition of power

Traditionally, power within an organization, especially among management or those in C-suite roles, has been perceived as an instrument of dominance and control. But what if leaders and managers started seeing their roles differently? Accepting oneness, justice, and love as the foundational premises on which our businesses must be built, can deeply *transform our view of power and authority.* We come to see these not as a tool to dominate and control but as conferring a duty upon leaders to foster an environment where everyone can thrive by fulfilling their individual potential and giving expression to their life's purpose and mission.

Congruent decision-making

Have you ever been at a crossroads, feeling torn between choices? These principles could serve as your North Star, ensuring your decisions resonate with your core values. This is as true in global governance as it is in corporate governance. For instance, when a nation decides to turn a blind eye to another nation's human rights abuses because they prioritize their needs to access the latter's energy, the long-term results for all nations are grave. Rooted in the trifecta of principles articulated here, we can chart a course that honors both imperatives. These principles, far from being abstract ideals, can serve as tangible guides for building systems and processes of corporate and societal governance that are ethical and life-enhancing.

Harmonious workplaces

By embracing the principles of oneness, justice, and love, leaders in business and government can witness a transformative shift in workplace dynamics. As individuals feel valued and appreciated, the work atmosphere evolves from one of resentment to one replete with enthusiasm and creativity. Recognizing everyone's contributions not only fosters a sense of ownership on the part of all, but also replaces negative emotions, such as anger, frustration, and blame, with a desire to leverage one's gifts and work in harmony with others towards a unified vision. In this revitalized environment, there's no need for micromanagement; teams naturally come together, driven by shared goals and requiring minimal guidance.

A more anchored perspective

The principles of oneness, justice, and love can be regarded as universal laws governing our social existence. Think of them as akin to the law of "gravity" that governs our physical existence. Just as we wouldn't dream of designing an airplane without considering gravity, so, too, we would be foolish to ignore these foundational principles when building our organizations, as we would be dooming them to collapse.

Consultation: a practical expression of the principle of justice

At this point, you might be wondering: *These principles sound great, but how do I actually put them into practice? How can these principles be applied in the business setting?*

Expressing love, oneness, and especially justice in a practical setting is achieved using the tool of consultation. Consultation happens when two or more individuals come together to discover the truth of a given situation, with the goal of arriving at an understanding and/or a decision that serves the collective good. During consultation all team members are invited to voice their opinions openly, honestly, and without fear of judgment. The emphasis is on the free exchange of ideas, taking care not to give offense but also understanding no one has the right to take offense. In such an environment the clash of diverse opinions (rather than egos), gives rise to the spark of truth. This process when faithfully followed benefits businesses, families, and any group that practices it, as it fosters a culture of understanding rather than a culture of clashing egos. When applied in business, everyone in the business feels involved in its growth and in shaping its direction leading to an overall sense of ownership. Moreover, studies have shown that this collective approach harnesses the creativity and insights of a diverse group, leading to better outcomes, including financial ones.

Let's break down some of the essential ingredients for a successful consultation:

- **Open expression:** every participant should be free to share their views fully, frankly and respectfully.
- **Detachment:** once shared, the individual lets go of his/her idea, which now belongs to the group.
- **Seeking truth:** the goal of the consultation is to arrive at the truth that serves the collective rather than a few individuals. Through the clash of diverse opinions, new insights often emerge.
- **Inclusivity:** every voice matters, regardless of rank, role, personality, or background.
- **Diversity:** the more diverse the group, the better: a varied group leads to richer discussions and better outcomes. It enhances collective understanding by allowing all participants to explore the many facets of the gem of truth.

Effective consultation captures the essence of ethical business practices, where love, justice, and oneness converge, allowing voices to unite, decisions to radiate integrity, and businesses to become catalysts for a brighter future. At the same time, consultation truly flourishes when each individual contributes with genuine authenticity, their distinctive capacities, and gives expression to their fullest potential. The foundation for building stronger organizations lies in showing up as our true selves and nurturing the skills essential for collective growth and success.

UNLEASH YOUR UNIQUE POTENTIAL FOR A MORE ETHICAL WORKPLACE

Stepping into a workplace ought to feel like stepping into an orchestra: every employee is akin to a musician playing in that orchestra – each contributes their unique sound, with passion, precision, and excellence. Just as an orchestra thrives on the varied capabilities and qualities of sound of its instruments, so, too, a business flourishes with the diverse talents, skills, and qualities of its members. When each team, or section of the orchestra, tunes its instruments to perfection and collaborates harmoniously, playing from the same score under the guidance of a single conductor, the result is a melodious symphony – a value-driven contribution that benefits and uplifts society at large.

And guess who the conductor of this orchestra is? Managers. A manager has the duty to create the conditions and guidance that allow individuals in their teams to discover and harness their unique strengths, ensuring their contributions are harmonious and impactful. If we accept the premise that businesses are the crucibles where our characters are forged, then it stands to reason that they are a key arena where we can best actualize our life's mission. Organizations and communities, in their ideal form, should therefore be nurturing environments that enable each of us to unlock and realize our fullest potential. At the same time, creating ethical conditions isn't solely the responsibility of organizations; individuals, too, have a pivotal role to play by genuinely bringing their true selves and contributing their authentic capabilities or "sounds". This isn't just a figment of our imagination – it's the magic of understanding one's distinctive capabilities.

Honoring your true path

Let me share a personal story that changed the way I thought of my own life's work: shortly after our wedding, my husband and I embarked on a honeymoon to the picturesque town of Siena in Tuscany, Italy. Like many young couples, we were grappling with decisions about our future, particularly the question of how many children we should have. I was torn, feeling guilty about wanting just one child while my husband envisioned a family of three. I questioned my desires, wondering if I was being selfish.

As fate would have it, during our stay in Siena, we ended up in a charming art gallery. While we were admiring the art, the artist entered and approached us, intent on striking up a conversation. He invited us upstairs to his family's apartment and then, with an intensity in his eyes, sat us down and began to share his own story. He spoke of having been born and raised in Siena which was governed by some firm societal expectations. Here, families typically had eight or nine children. When he and his wife married, he expressed a desire to have only one child, because he knew that having a large family would divert precious focus and energy away from his art, which, he believed, was his true life's calling. I still remember exactly what he told me: *"Never feel guilty for the choices you make in pursuit of your true calling. Sometimes, God puts us on this planet to make unique contributions. We can't dilute our energy too much; and that's ok."*

His words resonated deeply within me, providing me the clarity I was seeking about my purpose and mission, allaying my doubts and assuaging my guilt. It was as if the Universe had sent him to shed much-needed clarity in a moment of doubt and confusion. Some might say this guidance came in a bizarre way, but to me, it was a defining moment, a welcome sign that illuminated my path forward. In consultation with my husband, we chose to have just one child, in large measure so I could also dedicate myself to making contributions outside the home. I gave myself the permission to devote my time and energy to pursuing my self-identified mission of attempting to be a catalyst for individual and societal transformation; work I've been doing for the past twenty-four years.

Our unique potential

We are all endowed with a unique potential, waiting to be realized through the application of our volition. Life offers us a spectrum of experiences – some smooth, others challenging. One way or another, they all serve as opportunities for growth. It is also a fact that we are all constrained in one way or another by our life circumstances. There are elements in each of our lives we simply cannot control: whether we are born into a disadvantaged village, whether we face physical challenges like deafness, or whether we are born as girls in a place where female potential is undervalued. These are the threads of our existence with which we are born – some are as delicate as silk, others as rugged as wool. Some threads are multi-colored and shine brilliantly, while others are a dull gray. Yet, it's not the threads themselves, but the tapestry we weave from them for which we bear responsibility. More importantly, it is that tapestry that defines us and reflects who we have become. We might not have chosen these threads, but the design, the pattern, *the reality we create with them is entirely in our hands.*

This brings us to a profound realization: our worth isn't determined by external measures, but by how fully we realize our inherent potential. What matters is how well we apply our volition to actualize it. Consider our life's journey: one person might have the capacity of a bucket, another one that of a *bathtub*, and yet someone else the vastness of a *river.* In our society's bizarre perspective, we find ourselves comparing these capacities. For instance, in a maths class one student might receive a grade of C+ while another earns an A. But if the first student, with their bucket-sized capacity, has filled it to the brim, they've *achieved* 100% of *their potential and should be lauded for it.* By contrast, if the second student has a bathtub's worth of potential but only fills half of it, they have failed to truly realize their capabilities, even if, in sheer volume, the volume of their achievement surpasses that of their classmate's.

Unfortunately, our misunderstanding of the purpose of life has caused us to erroneously impose judgement on our inherent and natural differences in capacity. We use this judgement both to beat ourselves up and to denigrate others with devastating results. These natural differences in capacity become our excuse to inject two pervasive toxins in the business environment: *comparison and competition.* The whispers of *"She got the promotion, and I didn't"* or *"He's always handed the better projects"* echo in the corridors of our working places, breeding discontent. This constant vigilance, and perception of colleagues as competitors, erodes the spirit of collaboration, destroys our joy, robs us of motivation and energy, and decimates our sense of self-worth.

Yet, when we shift our perspective, recognizing that each individual's capacity is distinct and incomparable, we liberate ourselves from these self-imposed chains. No longer do promotions or accolades define our success let alone our self-worth; instead, it is the extent to which **we are fulfilling our unique potential that matters**. By embracing this understanding, we foster an environment of collaboration, mutual respect, encouragement and mutual growth. We can facilitate this spirit of collaboration by the simple act of reframing our perspective and seeing business as an opportunity to leverage our individual gifts in pure **service to the world**.

OUR DUAL *PURPOSE* IN LIFE: GROWTH AND CONTRIBUTION

"Humanity is on a common journey
in which all are protagonists."
The Universal House of Justice
(Global Governing Council of the Bahá'í Community)

"What is my purpose in life?" You've probably asked yourself this question at least once. Let's consider another analogy: that of a fetus in its mother's womb. Its primary task is to develop its limbs and organs for its life outside the womb. Even though it doesn't comprehend the 'why' behind this development – why develop eyes in darkness or legs in confinement? – it's imperative to do so. Otherwise, upon birth, it finds itself unprepared. Similarly, our journey is about nurturing qualities like honesty, truthfulness, kindness, and justice. It's about striving to be the best version of ourselves thereby evolving individually and collectively and contributing to an ever-advancing civilization. Understanding this gives us clarity as to what is, in my view, our dual purpose in life: firstly, to grow as individuals, continually refining our character, and secondly, to use our capacities to serve others and contribute to the well-being, peace, and betterment of the world. This ethos should permeate every facet of our lives, including our professional endeavors as we travel, shoulder-to-shoulder on a common journey towards a common goal.

If one of the key purposes we all share as human beings is to develop certain human qualities that are indispensable to becoming the best version of ourselves then we might well ask: what, if anything, makes us unique?

DEFINING YOUR MISSION: TAPPING INTO YOUR INNATE STRENGTHS

It's not what you do, it's who you become
(Jim Rohn)

While it's true that we all share a common purpose, yet each of us has a personal **mission in service of which we leverage our distinctive capacities and strengths**. I am sure we all remember the moment in which we asked ourselves: *"Which school should I attend?"*, *"Which internship will benefit me the most?"*, or *"How can I get that promotion to elevate my status?"*. What if instead we took the advice of the famous American entreprenuer, Jim Rohn, and posed a deeper, more introspective question: *" Who am I becoming?"* and *"Do I like the person I'm becoming?"* If the answer doesn't resonate with our core, it's time to move on. This is a good way to become and stay aligned with our individual mission.

While trying to understand what our mission is, it's crucial not to confuse mission with *career*: this is where much of our troubles arise. Career is merely a line of action among several potential lines of action through which we can fulfill our mission. When we view our mission as the application of our unique talents and strengths in service to a greater good, we realize our mission can be expressed in a myriad ways: through our chosen profession, our art, our writing, or even the noble task of parenting.

Recognizing and embracing our mission is liberating. It frees us from the torment of doubt, from the constant questioning of our path. More importantly, it empowers us to chart our own course, rather than letting others dictate it for us.

Unlocking our distinctive capabilities

The first step towards crafting our mission is identifying our distinctive capabilities. Each of us has a set of such capabilities; no one is bereft of them. They can, however, be easy for us to miss as often, our most profound strengths are so innate that we might overlook them, much like we take our ability to breathe for granted. These capabilities consist of the skills, strengths, talents, and passions that invigorate us, keeping our enthusiasm alive regardless of the hours or years we dedicate to them. Not only do they energize us, but they also inspire those around us. The beauty of these distinctive capabilities is that they offer us endless avenues for growth. We never reach a point where we may think *"I've been at this for 15 years; it's time to stop"*.

What is a distinctive capability?

Dan Sullivan, a renowned strategic thinker and coach, has identified the following key determinants of a distinctive capability. For something to qualify as your distinctive capability all four of these elements must be present:

- Something you do better than anyone else, that comes naturally to you.
- Something you are passionate about, that you never get bored with.
- Something that energizes both you and those around you.
- Something you can always improve at.

In what way does finding your distinctive capabilities and identifying your mission in life uplift your workplace?

- Individuals contribute their passions and strengths towards shared objectives.
- A surge in enthusiasm, passion, and positive energy is unlocked.

- Underperformance, a root of unhappiness, is minimized.
- The primary motivators become personal growth and value creation.
- Negative emotions like guilt and frustration diminish, uplifting the overall energy.
- Harmony is achieved by eliminating emotional and psychological barriers.
- Everyone aligns with their true capabilities, reducing internal conflicts.
- Minimal management is needed; just clear direction.

When everyone at work is aligned with their passions and strengths and consequently with their unique mission, and they spend their days giving expression to that mission, we witness a collective drive and positive motivation powered by the desire both to grow and to contribute meaningfully. This isn't just about improving business metrics; it's about elevating the human experience at work. As we close this chapter, remember that the key to a thriving workplace lies in recognizing and harnessing the unique value each individual brings.

Why is this topic so important to me and perhaps even to you?

Discovering my mission, rooted in my distinctive capabilities, became my North Star. This clarity not only shaped my career choices but also liberated me from societal pressures, especially those around motherhood. For me, this exercise was a key component of a journey of self-discovery. Perhaps, it will resonate with you too.

By 21, I was a lawyer, and after 15 years, found myself at the zenith of my career, part of a cadre of lawyers advising the US Government on the international law implications of its foreign policy decisions. Then came the gift of motherhood. After giving birth to my daughter, I interviewed numerous nannies and observed that none seemed genuinely interested in her well-being, but rather in their salary and benefits. I realized that while *many could be lawyers, only I could be her mother.*

The decision to leave my job was a heart-wrenching one. I grappled with a deep loss of identity and feelings of isolation; I questioned my choices daily. The world was used to seeing and defining me a particular way: as an international lawyer working in a prestigious workplace, but internally, I was in turmoil. It took courage to admit that beneath the accolades, I was deeply unhappy at work.

This introspection led to a profound realization: contrary to popular belief, life isn't a linear path but a series of choices designed to maximize our ability to grow and contribute. Moreover, while our careers might shift, our mission, if accurately identified, remains consistent. For me, it was time to take responsibility for my growth and transition from serving as an international lawyer to a mode of expressing my mission. I debunked the myth that careers are like trains on fixed tracks: life is about growth and leveraging our unique capabilities in service to the creation of a better the world, whether that's within our family, community, or globally.

This epiphany initially led me to a far more rewarding dual expression of my mission: raising our daughter while also contributing to the development of a new system of Global Governance. The latter work included writing five books, teaching numerous classes, delivering hundreds of lectures and worskshops and appearing on numerous TV and radio programs. When I eventually found myself missing the magic of witnessing the personal transformation arising from one-on-one connections with individuals as opposed to societal transformation, I trained as a life mastery coach. I thus added a third line of action, continuing to leverage my distinctive capabilities in service to my mission. Ultimately, all three paths aligned with my mission, allowing me to utilize my distinctive capabilities and navigate seamlessly between them. I learned that we truly are like musical instruments. Once we fine-tune our distinctive capabilities we can choose our performance setting: occasionally we may perform solo, at other times as part of an ensemble, and occasionally as part of an orchestra. Regardless of the context of our contributions, we remain true to our core mission.

TIPS FOR YOU

1) Discovering your distinctive capabilities is worth your time and energy.

This is a key that will give you the clarity you need for making career choices in life.

My suggestions for how you can start your journey of discovery follows:

- Talk to your friends, colleagues, family, and ask them to tell you, in as much detail as possible, what they view as your distinctive capabilities.
- Put all the feedback together and identify the areas of overlap: this is a great starting point to identify your distinctive capabilities.

2) Practice radical honesty with yourself.

Don't wait for a crisis to force you into action. When you find that you are unhappy, look your reality squarely in the eye, because your unhappiness is a signal that something isn't working and you need to change direction. It is not a sign of failure – a common misconception – in reality, a disempowering story we tell ourselves – that holds us back from making the changes we need to make.

If your thoughts are *"I hate my job, my boss, and my colleagues"* all this means is that you are likely not in the right environment to continue developing your potential. You have probably stagnated. Most of us think: *"if I am unhappy at work there must be something wrong with me"* and then they sink into depression or low-self esteem. Instead, think of it as the Universe telling you that you need to change direction. Regard this inner turmoil as an opportunity, not a failure. If you don't start making the changes, you can be sure the Universe will eventually force you into making them – this usually results in a more drastic and painful experience. So, don't wait; seize the day and take full respomsibility for shaping your own reality now!

CHALLENGING QUESTIONS

- What do you conceive of as your purpose in life?
- What do you conceive of as your distinctive capabilites?
- What is your mission in life?
- Is your current job leveraging your distinctive capabilities?
- What sort of relationships do you have with your colleagues and your managers? Do they mesh with your vision of what you want?
- Do you have regular opportunities for group consultations in your office? If not, could you propose or create such opportunities?

ABOUT THE AUTHOR

Sovaida Ma'ani Ewing is a prolific author, speaker, and international lawyer with 20 years' experience. She is the founding director of The Center for Peace and Global Governance (cpgg.org), a virtual think tank and online forum that pools and proposes principled solutions to pressing global challenges. She has written five books on peace and global governance; the latest is "The Alchemy of Peace." She also hosts a video podcast "Re-Imagining Our World" on the CPGG YouTube channel.

The Jesuit Blueprint: Shaping Organizational Identity and Culture

Eugenio Fernández-Dussaq

—

CFO & Co-Founder — BSmooth
Director of the Entrepreneur Lab
and Professor at NewU University

*"Act as if everything
depended on you;
trust as if everything
depended on God."*

Ignatius of Loyola

Saint Ignatius of Loyola founded the Society of Jesus (Jesuits) in 1540 and served as its first Superior General. Born in 1491 to a noble Basque family in Spain, Ignatius underwent a profound spiritual conversion while recovering from a war injury. This inspired him to dedicate his life to serving God and others.

After studying theology in Paris, Ignatius gathered a small group of companions who took vows of poverty, chastity, and obedience. They offered themselves to the Pope to go wherever he thought they could be most helpful. Approved by Pope Paul III in 1540, the Jesuits multiplied, known for their scholarship, discipline, and foreign missions.

Under Ignatius' leadership, the Jesuits were highly organized and systematic. He devised the Spiritual Exercises and wrote the Jesuit Constitutions, which formed the Society's core principles and procedures. Central values included obedience, adaptability, discernment, education, and inculturation.

The Jesuits played a significant role in the Counter-Reformation and spread Christianity globally through Asia, Africa, and the Americas. Education became a critical means for their mission. By Ignatius' death in 1556, 1000 Jesuits were running 35 schools.

Centuries later, this growth and enduring influence highlights how Ignatius' foresight in designing Jesuit Identity and Culture contributed to their success. Examining his approach offers insights applicable to modern organizations seeking to build sustainable, values-driven institutions.

The ingenious strategies of Ignatius of Loyola in founding the Society of Jesus in the 16th century reveal valuable insights into two vital concepts for organizations today: Identity and Culture. Though formulated centuries before these ideas were defined, Ignatius's intuitive understanding of the centrality of purpose, adaptability, and alignment in building a robust institution has much to teach modern leaders. Examining the Jesuits' Organizational Identity and Culture allows us to apply timeless principles to guide contemporary organizations. Crafting an intentional Identity provides a North Star for decisions and actions.

Cultivating an aligned culture gives Identity tangible expression through habits and behaviors. Wise leaders recognize that organizational endurance depends on nurturing these foundational elements. In a dynamic world, organizational Identity and Culture remain essential guides to channel collective effort toward a meaningful shared vision.

When starting an organization, we often establish a purpose and a structural base, just as St. Ignatius did in the Society. However, these crucial elements sometimes fall by the wayside because they must be effectively communicated and managed by those who would bring the institution to life through their daily work. In other words, an adequate culture that aligns people with the organization's purpose, values, and structure must still be developed. Ignatius should have avoided this, and it is his key to success.

KEY CONCEPTS

Organizational Identity refers to the central, distinctive, and enduring characteristics that define what an organization stands for. It includes purpose, values, Culture, history, symbols, and practices. Identity captures the organization's essence – what makes it unique. A strong, clearly defined Identity provides direction and guides decisions.

Organizational Culture consists of the shared assumptions, norms, behaviors, and values that shape how things are done in an organization. It's "the way we do things around here." Culture reflects and reinforces Identity through the habits, attitudes, and unwritten rules members adopt. A well-aligned culture translates Identity into action.

Discernment is carefully considering options to make wise, prayerful decisions. It involves reflecting with an open mind, evaluating using reason and intuition, and listening for inner guidance. Discernment aims to determine the best course of action by weighing pros, cons, and alignment with values.

The Jesuits were known for their discernment practices when making decisions. Their Spiritual Exercises prepared members to listen to their conscience and be receptive to God's will. Discernment enabled flexible, values-aligned choices.

Now that we've defined these foundational concepts, we can better appreciate how Ignatius of Loyola effectively integrated Identity, Culture, and discernment when forming the Jesuits. This provides helpful models for modern organizations building sustainable, meaningful institutions.

THE JESUIT ORGANIZATIONAL CULTURE

Although it was more than 400 years before the concept of Organizational Culture was created and developed, Ignatius' intuition was incredible when designing and constructing the Constitutions. According to some authors, the term' organizational culture' was first coined by Dr. Elliott Jaques in 1951, although others point out that Edgar Schein defined and classified it in the 1980s.

Organizational Culture refers to the values, beliefs, habits, and behaviors that characterize a human group within a company or institution. It is a set of intangible aspects that make up the organization's Identity and influences its members' decision-making behavior and how they relate.

Jesuits call organizational Culture our way of "proceeding," Although these are different terms, they refer to the same thing. We can see how certain attitudes, habits, and behaviors are developed in the Constitution to ensure that this "way of proceeding" is maintained over time as a distinctive element of being a Jesuit. Let us look at some of them:

1. **Obedience:** One of the fundamental principles of the Constitution is obedience to the superior of the order and the established norms. Jesuits must submit to the authority of their superiors and fulfill their duties and responsibilities.
2. **Formation:** The Constitutions establish a rigorous formation system for Jesuits, which includes studies in theology, philosophy, and humanities, as well as spiritual and apostolic practices.
3. **Collaboration:** Collaboration and teamwork are essential in order and with other individuals and organizations. Jesuits seek to work together for the common good and to meet the challenges of today's world.

4. **Discernment:** The Society of Jesus values discernment and making essential decisions through prayer, reflection, and dialogue. Jesuits seek to listen to the voice of God in their lives and the situations in which they work.
5. **Adaptability:** The Constitution emphasizes the importance of adapting to the changing circumstances and needs of Society and the church. Jesuits must be flexible and willing to modify their apostolate and community life according to the moment's demands.
6. **Inculturation:** Cultural diversity seeks to adapt to the circumstances and needs of the places where it works. Inculturation implies respecting and valuing local cultures and working with people in their context. Although St. Ignatius did not use the term "inculturation" in his writings and Constitutions, it is evident that the theological content of this concept is present in his work.
7. **Cura personalis:** This term, of recent origin in the Society of Jesus, refers to the personal and pastoral care given to each individual during formation and spiritual development. Coming from Latin, it means "attention to the whole person." Within the Society of Jesus, the uniqueness of each person is valued, and attention is given to their specific needs throughout their formation. This encompasses not only the spiritual dimension but also the emotional, social, and psychological dimensions of the individual. As with inculturation, the theological content of *cura personalis* is implicit, even if it is not directly mentioned. The concept of *institutional cura, which refers to the care and attention given to the organization or institution itself, is also incorporated.*

The importance given to our *way of proceeding*, which essentially represents the organizational Culture of the Society of Jesus, is vital to understanding the sustained success of the Society of Jesus over time. Ignatius intuited that the Culture of the Society is the primary means by which Jesuit Identity is humanly manifested. Organizational Culture establishes the guidelines, norms, and values that guide the behavior and actions of collaborators, which in turn reflects the organizational Identity in the environment in which we operate.

The Society of Jesus's organizational Culture is fundamental to achieving its objectives. This is where the integration of Identity elements materializes. Perceived Identity can drive or hinder the achievement of a company's strategic objectives. When aligned with strategy, a strong Identity facilitates the execution of plans and adaptation to change, while a weak or conflicting Identity can hinder implementation and the achievement of results.

One of the least recognized things about the Society of Jesus has been its ability to expand rapidly. We are talking about the fact that the Constitutions of the Society of Jesus were approved by the Pope in 1550, and 50 years later, at the beginning of the 17th century, the Jesuits were already covering Europe, America, Africa, and Asia. All this at a time when transporting from one place to another could take months.

Today, despite all the transportation and communication facilities, the thought of global expansion creates a headache for anyone.

Many companies can only dream of reaching all the markets that the Jesuits covered. But again, the genius of St. Ignatius stands out. He designed the Society to be a worldwide organization from the beginning. Adaptability, inculturation, and cura personalis were indispensable attitudes to achieve the expansion of Society in such an accelerated way. These values can only be assimilated and used effectively in a living organization. That is why, among other reasons, it takes so much time to be formed as a Jesuit.

Now, I want to delve deeper into the theme of discernment. We know that it is crucial for St. Ignatius that one learns to make the right decisions, that is, to have "critical thinking." Critical thinking is a concept that has been introduced previously. Its origin goes back to ancient Greece and its great philosophers Socrates, Plato, and Aristotle. Although it was not them, the philosopher Max Black, credited with the term's paternity, used it as the title of a book on logic in 1946. Critical thinking is an intellectual process that involves analyzing, evaluating, and synthesizing information thoughtfully and systematically. It is a skill that allows us to understand, interpret, and evaluate ideas and arguments objectively, logically, and rigorously.

In the world we live in, where Artificial Intelligence will begin to replace many jobs that require some training and robotics is replacing jobs that did not, the outlook for the future is cloudy. What is clear to me is that the jobs available in the future will be held by people who can be discerning and use their critical judgment.

I suspect that the differentiation of companies will be based on a single element: the critical judgment that the staff brings to the institution. The rest will be generated by AI, Robotics, Virtual Reality, and all the technologies we have at our disposal. Remember what the RAE says about Culture: "Set of knowledge that allows someone to develop their critical judgment." In other words, personnel with a solid organizational culture can only develop their critical judgment and contribute to what companies will require in the future. It should be noted that most organizations only value the crucial assessment of a few employees, thus wasting essential resources. For this reason, they have not designed a strategy to learn about and encourage the critical judgment of the people who work with them.

ORGANIZATIONAL IDENTITY

Identity is one of the fundamental pillars of human life. A mental, psychological, and spiritual structure defines our Identity, beliefs, customs, and relationships with others. This structure, rooted in our psychology and history, is so robust that, when threatened, it can lead a person to risk and sacrifice his life in defense of what he considers his own and the values that sustain it. Without taking a political position in such a conflict, today, the Ukrainians provide us with a clear example of this.

In the previously written book, we argue that organizational Identity is the only sustainable differentiating strategy. By analyzing the works of Michael Porter and other contemporary authors, we conclude that the core of the strategy lies in being different and understanding why we make decisions. A well-defined and managed Identity makes us unique, representing our organizational DNA. Just as no two people are alike, no two organizations are alike when their unique Identity is designed and preserved.

Today, I argue that organizational Identity is the integration of these five key elements:

1. **Purpose**
2. **Values**
3. **Organizational Culture**
4. **Founding structure and regulations**
5. **Marks and badges**

In addition, other elements make up organizational identities, such as symbols, beliefs, traditions, objectives, attributes, and practices. Identity is the structure of the essence of each organization and its personality and reflects how it perceives itself and how others perceive it.

When Ignatius of Loyola designed the Identity of the Society of Jesus, he designed it to be time- and people-proof. For two decades, Ignatius devoted time and effort to building this Identity of the Society of Jesus. Although he did not know the concept itself, he sensed its indispensability.

Organizational Identity gained prominence in the academic literature thanks to researchers Albert and Whetten (1985), who proposed a clear definition of it as "those attributes that are central, distinctive and enduring in an organization." Since then, the concept has evolved and expanded, giving rise to various theoretical and empirical approaches that explore how organizations construct, maintain, and change their Identity over time.

It is essential to clarify that organizational Identity works in any institution. Still, public and private entities with operational or business units of such dimension must develop strategic teams for each.

If we apply these concepts to the case of the Society, we find that its purpose is to attain "Christian perfection, their own and that of others, for the glory and service of God." Although they did not initially see themselves as educators – the ultimate purpose of the Jesuits was the salvation of souls – they soon realized that education was an appropriate strategy to achieve their purpose. Their strategic educational units aim for their students to be "men and women for others," which aligns with the ultimate aim. Its purpose became more specific in the case of Liceo Javier de Guatemala. It was to "be men and women at the service of others in the way of Jesus." These purposes of the strategic units are indispensable to creating a particular Identity but always adhere harmoniously to the totality of the Society, as should happen with multinationals.

Organizational Identity is so elemental to achieving success and sustaining it over time that it is surprising how little it has been studied and how little attention is given to it.

Organizational Identity is the underlying structure that determines people's behavior within any institution. When this Identity is not clearly defined, it becomes a mosaic that intertwines leaders' identities with other latent structures. Some describe it as silos, where the Identity of each silo manifests itself, which can result in diverse behaviors. A solid and well-defined organizational Identity is essential to ensure the alignment of its members' values, objectives, and actions, facilitating collaboration and achieving common goals.

ORGANIZATIONAL CULTURE AS AN EXPRESSION OF ORGANIZATIONAL IDENTITY

Organizational Culture is the human manifestation of organizational Identity. This human manifestation can be observed in the first dimension, habits and attitudes, but needs to be clarified in the second dimension, which encompasses role Identity and group Identity.

The most visible layer of organizational Culture is a realm defined by habits and attitudes. This layer is akin to the surface of a vast ocean, where the actions and interactions of the organization's members are openly displayed. In this context, habits are akin to the repeated strokes of a swimmer – consistent, patterned behaviors that employees exhibit routinely, like the systematic organization of a workspace or the structured approach to meetings. Conversely, attitudes are the undercurrents that influence these actions – the mental and emotional stances that color perceptions and reactions to the work environment. They are the sentiments that shape whether an employee approaches a task with enthusiasm or reluctance. In this observable realm, habits manifest as actions are taken, while attitudes reveal how these actions are executed. This dimension should be designed and managed accordingly. Its tangible actions and visible behaviors offer a clear window into understanding an organization's Culture, contrasting the more elusive, profound elements of a person's Identity.

A different concept of organizational Identity is a personal Identity. There are multiple dimensions, perspectives, and approaches to human Identity. Some researchers have proposed classifications based on different types of Identity.

Although there is no single universally accepted classification, one of the standard classifications focuses on three main types of Identity that impact organizational Identity:

1. **The Identity of the role**
2. **Group Identity**
3. **The Identity of the person**

Role Identity refers to the multiple meanings that define a person's Identity based on their various societal roles, the groups to which they belong, and their characteristics. Individuals coexist within a social structure and, throughout their lives, play different roles, such as student, worker, or spouse. These roles provide structure, organization, and meaning to the person and the situation.

Role Identity is the internalized meaning of a role that individuals apply to themselves. For example, a coach's role Identity may include the meaning of mentor and friend, while a manager's role Identity may include the importance of leader and supervisor. Role Identities acquire meaning from the Culture and individuals' unique interpretations of the role. Therefore, different people may attribute different meanings to the same role Identity, leading to confusion, disorientation, and conflict.

At the organizational level, its members must clearly understand their roles. The role is not simply a job description; it goes beyond that, as it implies each individual's personal significance and contribution to the institution. Most organizations must adequately address the importance of defining and managing roles, which can lead to alignment and commitment problems.

Group Identity refers to an individual's sense of belonging to a specific group and how they identify with it. Group Identity influences a person's self-esteem and sense of connection to Society. In organizations, individuals who do not feel they belong or do not identify with the group have difficulty aligning with the organizational Identity and contributing effectively.

Concise, positive, and precise group Identity is vital to success in any organization. With it, sustainable success is possible. It is important that members feel connected and committed to the group rather than feeling like mere tools in the workplace.

Personal Identity implies seeing oneself as a unique and distinctive individual, different from others. In the organizational context, personal Identity represents the individual attributes and characteristics that enable each member to bring something unique and further to the organization.

Organizations must foster a balance in which members embrace and identify with the roles and values of the group but, at the same time, maintain and value their characteristics and skills. This allows for greater diversity, innovation, and resilience within the organization while preserving cohesion and a sense of belonging to a joint group.

The second dimension, role and group Identity, encompasses the internal and personal perceptions of organizational members about themselves concerning their specific roles and group membership. Role Identity focuses on how individuals interpret and understand their organizational roles and responsibilities. On the other hand, group Identity relates to how employees identify and connect with a specific group within the organization. This dimension is less visible, as it refers to internal and subjective aspects that are only sometimes readily observable.

Habits and attitudes are more evident and directly observable, and role and group Identity are more subtle and are based on internal perceptions and experiences of individuals in the organization. These two dimensions interact and influence each other, contributing to the construction and expression of organizational Culture.

Considering that organizational Culture is designed and executed to support the values and purposes of the organization, culture management from the two dimensions mentioned (habits and attitudes and role and group Identity) must be aligned with those values and purposes. Here are some strategies to achieve this:

1. **Habits and attitudes:**
   a) Ensure that values and purposes are communicated to all employees: Sharing and constantly reinforcing the organization's values and purposes helps employees internalize them and reflect them in their habits and attitudes.
   b) Implement training and development programs that reinforce values and purpose: Training and development programs should be designed to promote skills, behaviors, and attitudes aligned with the organization's values and purposes.
   c) Plan, implement, and follow up on systems that promote the habits and attitudes that the organization will work on.

2. **Role and group Identity:**
   a) Align role expectations with the organization's values and purpose: When defining and communicating role expectations, ensure that they are aligned with the organization's values and purpose so that employees can see how their roles contribute to achieving those purposes.

b) Encourage collaboration and teamwork based on values and purposes: Team projects and activities should align with the organization's values and purposes, allowing collaborators to work together toward common goals and reinforce group Identity.

c) Facilitate leadership based on values and purpose: Organizational leaders should act as role models and champions of the organization's values and purposes, ensuring that their actions and decisions are aligned with these principles.

It is necessary to manage the organization's intangibles, such as Identity, human relationships, knowledge, and change, with the same impetus with which we manage all tangible assets. If we do not service a vehicle, it will fail until it stops working. The same is true of organizational Identity.

In the end, organizational Identity and Culture serve as pillars and pathways. Identity provides the solid foundation, the North Star anchoring an organization's sense of purpose and values. Culture paves the path, channeling collective effort through norms and behaviors aligned with Identity. When Identity rings clear and Culture reinforces it, organizations flourish. Leaders who harness these interconnected forces skillfully leave a legacy that stands the test of time.

Ignatius of Loyola exemplified mastery of Identity and Culture design centuries ago, forging an iconic institution that still thrives today. By learning from the Jesuits' wisdom in balancing crisp Identity with adaptive Culture, modern organizations can build a legacy made to last. Though terminology evolves, human values and psychology remain constant. Identity gives unique meaning, and Culture brings a shared vision to life. To build for the centuries, leaders must sculpt both elements carefully and help each stone support the next. When Identity and Culture align, ordinary groups become heroic organizations destined to make their mark on the world.

CHALLENGING QUESTIONS

- What action can you take to better align your personal values with your organization's?
- How can you use adaptability to enhance your service to others?
- What step will you take to incorporate more discernment into your decision-making?
- Identify one way you can embrace cultural diversity to improve outcomes.
- How will you apply 'cura personalis' to foster holistic care in your interactions?

ABOUT THE AUTHOR

Eugenio Fernández-Dussaq is a multifaceted man whose passion and experience span various disciplines and professional fields.

As a university professor, he has inspired his students to reach their full potential and has shared his knowledge and wisdom at numerous renowned institutions.

In addition to his academic work, Eugenio is a prolific author, businessman, and entrepreneur. He has developed innovative methodologies such as Management By Activity, revolutionizing how organizations approach management and decision-making.

As a speaker, Eugenio has shared his idea and experiences with audiences worldwide, distinguishing himself as a leader in his field.

Eugenio has also advised companies internationally, helping them grow and prosper in increasingly competitive markets. His hands-on approach and experience in business management make him a valuable resource for any organization seeking to improve its operations and achieve its goals.

Living in the United States, Eugenio, and his partner Carlos Reyes created a management platform called GoBsmooth. It is designed to help companies improve their performanceand manage their operations, aiming to help them achieve organizational 'magis'.

With his leadership and vision, Eugenio Fernández-Dussaq continues to make a lasting and marking business and education, contributing to the growth and success of organizations and the individuals within them.

Woman in Finance: Making Finance Work for Women – A Personal Journey

Shiva Dustdar

—

Director at the European Investment Bank, the EU Climate Bank, Head and Dean of EIB Institute Leader in Innovation and Sustainable Finance/ Speaker/ Change Agent/ Connector

*"It will come to pass that
when women participate
fully and equally in
the affairs of the world,
and when they enter
confidently and capably
the great arena of laws and
politics, war will cease; for
women will be an obstacle
and hindrance to it. This
is true and without doubt."*

'Abdu'l-Bahá,
*The Promulgation
of Universal Peace*

REPURPOSING FINANCE THROUGH A GENDER LENS

We live in a world designed by men for men, in our private lives, and at work. But we need to create and design a world built by humans for humans.

To do this, we must look at the world through a gender lens. Whenever we're analyzing, planning, or making a decision in terms of finance and business, we must always examine the implications on the lives of women and men.

My vision is led by a sense of duty toward women who aren't as fortunate as I am and a sense of gratitude to my grand-parents who believed in the value of education, especially of girls. My parents left Iran in the 1960s, searching for a better life. In my country of origin, women are denied even the most basic rights. I'm fortunate because although I grew up in an environment that isn't perfect for women, we do have fundamental human rights and growth opportunities. I benefited from a more egalitarian society, and I owe what I am today to the opportunities I had.

I started working in finance thirty years ago, in a very male-dominated environment at J.P. Morgan on Wall Street. After a few years, I noticed that my male colleagues were moving up the career ladder faster, and there were very few women in senior positions to look up to and get career advice from. Getting in wasn't the hard part. We were a diverse group, but the way the work was organized and the few female role models advocating diversity and inclusion meant that our career prospects were more limited, especially once we started having children.

When I moved to a publicly-owned international financial institution, I realized that the public sector wasn't either set up to value the talents of both men and women. If you didn't create an enabling environment that allowed staff to take care of their families and work, women would fall behind and the organization would lose valuable talent along the way.

In addition, career progression was mainly driven by seniority rather than meritocracy, creating further barriers for women to break into managerial posts. During my first ten years at the bank, I led and co-led our equal opportunity committee to help change our internal policies and attract more women executive staff. Our goal was to enable professional women to break through the managerial glass ceiling.

We improved our maternity and paternity leave policies, giving more time to couples to handle and manage their professional lives. We also introduced measures, such as the appointment of at least one woman in selection panels and external assessment centers for management positions to reduce gender bias in the selection process. Over time, we also introduced gender targets for administrative, executive and management staff and made them publicly available for closer monitoring.

In the last ten years, I have focused my attention externally on creating better access to finance for women entrepreneurs, including developing financial products and advisory services that can reach the whole society. This focus has been part of my bank's wider commitment to introduce a gender lens into its infrastructure and innovation investments.

How might we direct our investments to empower women rather than disadvantage them? What does it mean to bring in a gender lens to our investments?

For example, if we are financing a public transport project, such as subways, we take the following into account:

- Accessibility: women may be traveling with children, so it's important that the subway can be easily accessed with a stroller.
- Safety: women often travel alone and the environment must be safe and make them feel safe.
- Route planning: there must be stops in places where women work or where there are schools or children activities.

Similarly, let's consider urban planning. In the past, cities weren't built using a gender lens. Schools were often distant from workplaces because, typically, men went to work, while women took care of the children. Today, both men and women work, so there's a need for childcare to be closer to the workplace. Typical male working environments – like Wall Street in New York or other financial districts – have historically not had nearby childcare facilities.

Another example is that streets in many developing countries often have no sidewalks, making it dangerous for pedestrians to walk along the roads. It so happens that it is often women who walk long distances to fetch water and other necessities, placing them in danger. Hence, when our bank finances roads, it demands the project to include well-lit sidewalks for safe passage of pedestrians.

Today, when we redesign cities, not only do we want to reduce transport problems and CO2 emissions, but we also want the whole ecosystem around it to be more integrated. Bringing in a gender lens brings a new vision to urban and rural planning.

Until I read the eye -opening book "Invisible Women" by Caroline Criado Perez, I had not realized that product design is often gender biased, following the so- called " male default". Women are more likely to die in a car accident, because the car's safety features were tested on dummies of a male body. Similarly, in the past (and to some extent today), drugs, such as for cardiovascular diseases, weren't properly tested on women subjects during clinical trials. As a result, women have died from side effects that weren't identified during clinical trials. Women's health remains to this day one of the most under-researched areas, hence also offering some of the best investment opportunities.

When we make investments, we often don't consider that whatever we are financing – whether it is an infrastructure or innovation, - will impact women and men differently and these differences need to be understood and managed to avoid the "male-default" of the past.

Three pillars for an effective gender lens strategy

- We need a gender-smart investment approach that replaces the "male default" with a "human default".
- We need to ensure that women entrepreneurs have equal access to capital to start and scale their businesses.
- We need more women in key positions where investment decisions are made. Studies show that when women control checkbooks, those companies make more sustainable investments.They also have better ratings for governance and achieve higher financial returns, leveraging the diversity in their workforce. To enable women to be in top positions, we must look at how work is organized, where it takes place, what support mechanisms exist, and what incentives the company offers. Having more women in key financial positions who proactively support women entrepreneurs and bring in a gender lens to their investments, is of course a big first step towards a truly inclusive economic system.

But this isn't enough to simply place a few women in key positions. We need a holistic approach that starts with how we raise our boys and girls, ensuring equal opportunities and an enabling inclusive work environment where men and women prosper. The following quote from the Bahai writings puts it beautifully:

The world of humanity has two wings – one is women and the other men. Not until both wings are equally developed can the bird fly. Should one wing remain weak, flight is impossible.
Abdu'l-Bahá

Courage is needed because a gender lens places some of the fundamental principles of economics under question. Specifically, it questions the part of the economy that is often invisible, unpaid labor. This includes mothers taking care of their children and people, mostly women caring for the elderly. Work that doesn't have money associated with it, is not captured in our current economic system. Looking at a world where you bring in the full contributions by men and women whether they are paid or unpaid means rethinking what drives our economy.

Katrine Marçal in her book "Who cooked Adam Smith's dinner?" sheds light on the irony in Adam's Smith economic theory and his own life. For example, if you look at Adam Smith's fundamental premise in his economic theory, the baker or butcher acted in their self-interest to produce their products, but for them to be able to go to work, somebody had to take care of their children and household. Economists never acknowledged this often invisible, yet indispensable part of the economy. Our economic models must properly account for all elements that feed into our economies to avoid the flawed incentives and misallocation of resources in our current system.

Ironically, Adam Smith's mother took care of his everyday needs. He lived at home, and she took care of his food and clothes, so he could focus on his work and writing. She didn't do it because she was paid for it or obliged to do it, but because she loved him and wanted to take care of him.

However, love and care don't feature anywhere in our current economic system. Changing this will put this type of vision in a context of global challenges, related to climate change, the health crisis (was the pandemic a wake-up call?), and inequality in general. If you look at these global challenges, even though we have financial resources, our financial system has failed us or else, we would be tackling these challenges. The current setup – how decisions are made and who makes them – is failing us as a society. Thus, we are lurching from one crisis to another.

But poly-crises also generate poly-opportunities. These opportunities come from looking at the current economic and financial system and developing a new inclusive, world-embracing vision not only of the actors, but also of the work they do.

Current economic theories have failed to capture many hidden factors that enable production to happen and have created a system that doesn't allow the money to go where it's most needed. One way to start fixing our current financial system is to start using a gender lens when we analyze, plan, and make decisions. This is how inclusive finance can build a world by humans for humans.

How we did it and are still doing it.

When I joined the financial institution, I work for, I wanted to help entrepreneurs bring new ideas to life. But when we started setting up financing schemes for innovative companies, we discovered that many were not yet investment-ready and they needed additional support. We set up a dedicated advisory service to improve access to finance for such innovators. We helped them develop their business plans and prepare for their next financing rounds. What we however noticed was that most of the companies we advised were founded or led by men. This made us curious to find out why so few women-led companies approached us for financing.

We commissioned a market study to look at the access to finance conditions for women entrepreneurs in Europe, compared to US and Asia.

Our study "Funding women entrepreneurs – how to empower growth" (2020) offered some eye-opening and disheartening reality.

- Most women entrepreneurs were not aware of financing instruments available to them, especially those in the European Union funding programs.
- Only 2% of Venture Capital money went to women entrepreneurs, perhaps even less after the pandemic. Even though there's was a positive trend of more women founding or leading companies, there was still a big gap if you looked at how many companies were founded by women versus the number of companies being funded.
- About 30% of newly created companies were founded or led by women, suggesting that women-led companies faced higher financing barriers.

The study revealed there was a great potential to improve things and that public finance institutions had an important catalytic role to play. Rather than waiting for women entrepreneurs to find us, we decided to look for them proactively, offer them financial advice and guidance on which financial instrument was best suited to meet their needs.

The study also showed that the more women were involved in investment their decisions positions, the more money went to women-led companies. To accelerate change, we worked closely with associations of women in venture capital who were actively promoting women in key investment decision positions and amplified their call for change.

Our process involved three steps: – identifying - advising – and making sure projects had access to the various financing sources available This activity is ongoing and has brought a greater awareness in the market about the challenge and opportunities for gender - smart investing.

TIPS FOR MORE INCLUSIVE FINANCE

If we want to create a financial world fit for purpose, we need both men and women.

Often, when we offer seminars on gender smart investing, most of the audience is women. But as a society, we must realize that if we don't create a world that caters to the needs of both women and men, the first people to lose out are men.

My advice therefore is for everyone to bring in a gender lens into and ask themselves about any activity they are involved in:

How does this investment decision impact men and women? What does it mean to bring in a gender lens into this activity or decision? We tend to have blind spots, while we need to have mirrors.

We need to engage in networks outside our natural networks with people who are different from us. This offers an opportunity for growth; diversity creates opportunities.

My advice to young professionals is to build their careers by creating opportunities for establishing meaningful connections with diverse groups of people, both on a professional and a personal basis. The world today is so connected that chances are your paths cross again. The more you've nurtured a rich network of diverse people from different fields, the richer your experience of the world will be. And you'll be much more effective in whatever profession you're in. You can no longer afford to zoom in on your narrow field and ignore the rest.

We must all contribute toward the creation of a world where both women and men thrive and support each other to realize their full potential.

CHALLENGING QUESTIONS

- Look at the world surrounding you with a gender lens. What do you see?
- Do you know any women entrepreneurs? What was their path like?
- Have you ever felt penalized in your job because of your gender?
- What can you do to promote a more inclusive and diverse work environment around you?

ABOUT THE AUTHOR

Shiva Dustdar is an esteemed expert in innovation and sustainable finance with a 30-year track record in New York, London, and Luxembourg, serving at institutions like J.P. Morgan, Fitch Ratings, and the European Investment Bank (EIB). Renowned for her strategic and inclusive leadership, Shiva drives sustainable and digital economic transitions. At EIB, she has pioneered innovative financing instruments, like the Infectious Disease Finance Facility and has been at the helm of pivotal financing projects since 2003. She's a prominent voice in sustainable finance, currently leading the EIB Institute to align EIB's mission with societal goals through innovative and climate-focused collaborations.

Educated at Columbia University and London Business School, Shiva also co-founded the European High Yield Association, now a part of AFME, earning recognition as one of the Top 50 Women in Credit in 2006. Her leadership earned her the WIN - Women International Network Award in 2023.

Shiva balances her professional accomplishments with a fulfilling family life as a spouse and parent to two adult children.

It's Time to Clarify Your Vision and Spread It!

Denise Cumella

—

Empowering professionals and entrepreneurs to write, publish, and promote impactful business books. Leveraging 15+ years of marketing expertise and experience as an international bestselling author. Ebbf Board Member

"Books give a soul
to the universe,
wings to the mind,
flight to
the imagination,
and life
to everything."

Plato

The world yearns for businesses that prioritize *work-life balance, gender equality, and sustainable growth*. As a woman and a mother, the quest for a fulfilled career that doesn't compromise my family time or my values has been a personal battle, one that many of us face daily. Ethical businesses play a crucial role in this journey, offering a blueprint for a world where success is measured not just by profit, but by the *wellbeing* of its people. An ethical business is where work and personal life can not only coexist but also enrich each other, setting a new standard for what it means to truly succeed.

Starting my career with a multinational giant, I found a profound sense of fulfillment and purpose. Every project, every deadline, and every strategy meeting resonated with me, painting a picture of a career that was as rewarding as it was challenging. I was a great manager, rewarded and appreciated, with a promising professional path in front of me. However, this alignment of my professional aspirations and personal satisfaction encountered an unexpected crossroads the moment I embraced motherhood. Becoming a mother was a wake-up call. Suddenly, the clarity and coherence of my life's path were overshadowed by a stark dichotomy: the rigorous demands of being a top-tier manager versus the innate desire to be a present and nurturing parent. The endless meetings and continuous travels, the pressure to always be "on," and the expectation to put work before everything else didn't make sense anymore.

This realization hit me hard. I was at the top of my game professionally, but becoming a mother introduced a whole new set of priorities. There was this huge gap between the drive to excel professionally and the equally strong desire to be there for every milestone, every tear, and every laugh of my child's life. It felt like being pulled in two opposite directions, and something had to give. I was at a fork in the road: continue on the path laid out for me or forge a new one that aligned with my values and new role as a mother. The corporate world, with its rigid schedules and relentless demands, simply didn't fit into this new equation.

I did not take the decision to reinvent myself lightly. It involved a profound introspection and a bold willingness to step into the unknown. Choosing to start anew wasn't easy, but it was necessary. It was about building a future where I could be both a successful entrepreneur and a present, loving parent. So, I took everything I knew from my corporate days and poured it into starting my own business, with the aim of weaving together the profound joy and responsibility of motherhood with the deep satisfaction derived from a genuine and successful career. I reached out to colleagues who shared my vision and values, those brave enough to step into the uncertain world of startups with me. Together, we built a company grounded in the principles of ethical business. Our goal was to both create a successful enterprise and empower others to lead with integrity, balance, and purpose.

Our mission was clear: to inspire managers, professionals, and entrepreneurs to uncover and embrace the noblest aspects of their being. We aimed to be more than just a business; we aspired to be a beacon for those business people seeking to understand not just what they could offer the world, but who they truly wanted to be, to identify the precious gems within themselves and make them shine as they deserve.

With my story I want to underline the transformative power of personal growth and the courage to follow one's convictions. Choosing a different path from the one that makes sense and finding harmony between professional ambition and personal fulfillment means, ultimately, building a future where success is measured not just by achievements, but by the authenticity and integrity of one's journey. That is the reason why this path felt right for me. Today, my passion lies in doing the same for others; in my work, I thrive everyday on uncovering others' visions and their core motivations, connecting on a deeper level, and sharing the most authentic parts of ourselves to inspire and lead. Helping individuals clarify their vision and express it in a way that's both clear and accessible is the mission I continue to pursue in my daily life, with The Boss Books, my company.

IDENTIFY YOUR VISION AND MAKE YOUR VOICE ETERNAL

In today's world, making our presence known is essential – not just for the sake of visibility, but to connect and solve real problems people are facing. The digital landscape is vast, and everyone is searching online for solutions, for community, for inspiration. So, yes, we need to communicate to exist, to be discovered. But the real question is, *how do we wish to be perceived? What kind of energy do we want to emit?* How do we want our personal ethos, our brand, our team to be received? It's all about setting the tone for how we want to engage with the world and ensuring that every piece of content, every interaction, reflects the core of **who we are and what we stand for.**

Unfortunately, over time, many organizations find their core messages becoming diluted. This can happen as founders pass on and new individuals step in, leading to a loss of the original identity and the real soul of the project. Without this core, the project loses its appeal, because *the strongest asset of any organization* isn't just its products or services, but its **people, their talents, and their hidden stories**. In a world where talented individuals are in short supply, especially in Western societies where people seek meaningful work, maintaining a clear and compelling vision is vital. We need to continually remind our teams of the purpose behind their work and the *unique contribution* they're making to society, as alternatives are always just a click away.

Inside each of us lies something noble, a gem waiting to be shared. Too often, these treasures remain hidden, obscured by the bustle of daily toil or the whispers of doubt. Yet, their brilliance is undeniable. Our mission, our privilege, is to bring forth that noblest part of ourselves and make it available for others to witness, to be inspired by, and to act upon.

CRAFTING YOUR LEGACY: THE TRANSFORMATIONAL POWER OF PUBLISHING A BOOK

The act of writing is not just an intellectual exercise; it is a personal odyssey that hones your vision. Teaching and sharing are powerful tools for self-improvement; as we articulate our vision, we understand it more deeply and see the world through a new lens.

This process goes beyond communication – it's about ensuring that your communication serves a purpose and adds value to the lives of others.

This is where my love for assisting people in capturing and sharing their vision through books comes in. Many have a vision and the desire to make a positive impact, leveraging their skills for the greater good. Yet, without proper encouragement or a solid foundation, these visions can fade, weaken, or completely disappear over time. **Books serve as a powerful medium to preserve the essence of a project** or an individual's work, preventing it from becoming watered down. They anchor ideas in words, ensuring that these concepts last beyond the person's immediate influence, age, or geographical presence. This way, the vision continues to inspire and reach others, even if the original visionary never has the chance to interact with them directly.

Why should a person's voice be preserved eternally in a book?

- to maintain the integrity and **essence of our projects** over time
- so people can understand it, benefit from it, and be inspired **across generations**
- because **great ideas are valuable and deserve to last**, they should not get lost

My role is to ensure that the unique voices and visions of individuals are preserved and shared, providing eternal inspiration and making a lasting impact. My goal is to ensure that the essence of a project can be understood by anyone, in any context, even 50 years from now: it is a process of reconstructing their ideas to ensure they are understandable and appealing to people.

We all harbor noble ideas deserving of a wider audience: the mission I pursue is to unlock and amplify these ideas, ensuring they are accessible and can contribute to shaping public discourse and inspiring organizational change. When we initiate projects or launch organizations that hold significant value right from the start – be it a new business unit, an NGO, or a groundbreaking project – it is essential to share the origins of these endeavors: why we embarked on them, how we brought them to life, and what are the stories that fueled their inception?

What excites me the most is discovering those stories, engaging in meaningful conversations with individuals about their motivations and aspirations, diving into the heart of what gives their work purpose: the reason why they do what they do, the ultimate purpose of their work. This way, we're not just building businesses; we're fostering communities bonded by passion and a shared vision and creating a magnet for like-minded individuals.

Imagine how powerful it would be to surround ourselves with people who reflect our own energy and drive: to achieve this, we need to craft messages that resonate deeply and share them in ways that are both organized and impactful. Do you know what the greatest obstacle in doing this is? Ourselves. Our own hesitation to share these valuable insights, and the profound insights that could revolutionize our personal and professional worlds often remain unexpressed, buried within us due to our hectic schedules or reluctance to face potential scrutiny.

UNTANGLING CHRISTMAS LIGHTS

Think of clarifying ideas as the process of untangling Christmas lights. It's a vivid metaphor for the journey many embark upon when striving to articulate their visions, especially when dreaming of authoring their signature book. This act of unraveling is not just about being seen or understood; it's about feeling inspired to start the transformative work of publishing our book. People often grasp the essence of their own message but need assistance in refining it, in learning how to present it more coherently. This is where the magic happens, and it's precisely what my approach facilitates.

Imagine the all-too-familiar scenario: hastily packed away Christmas lights, a tangled mess stuffed into a box, only to emerge as a daunting knot the following year. Despite the tangle, the lights still glow when plugged in, but the real challenge lies in untangling each bulb, each idea, to reveal its full potential. My process is akin to patiently working through those knots, ensuring that each thought, each spark of brilliance, is given the space to shine.

When properly untangled, a single string of lights can illuminate an entire house, transforming it with warmth and radiance. Similarly, ideas, when meticulously unraveled and laid out, can light up not just a corner, but an entire landscape of thought. This transformation is at the heart of what I do: seeing beyond the jumble, recognizing the potential for beauty and impact in what may initially appear as a chaotic cluster of thoughts.

It's incredibly frustrating to sit with a mind full of ideas, unable to see how they connect or how they could be appreciated by a wider audience. My Bookcamp – the first step of my method – is designed to address this very frustration. It's about untangling those metaphorical Christmas lights of ideas, making sense of the mess, and laying out a clear, illuminated path forward. Just like a well-organized string of lights can transform the ambiance of a home, a well-structured book can captivate and engage readers far and wide, turning individual insights into a coherent, compelling narrative.

ELIMINATING THE FRUSTRATION OF HAVING LOTS OF IDEAS

Writing your book isn't just about putting words on paper; it's a transformational journey that reshapes you both professionally and personally. Here's the thing: embarking on the adventure of writing a book and crystallizing your vision is more than an act of creation; it's a profound journey of self-discovery and growth. It starts with taking a deep dive into your own experiences, examining what you do, and pinpointing areas for improvement. Teaching, in essence, becomes a powerful tool for self-enhancement. Through the process of articulating your thoughts and sharing your knowledge, you gain insights into what works, what doesn't, and how you can elevate your approach. This pattern of strategic reflection encourages authors to delve into the essence of who they are, uncover the impactful messages they possess, and contemplate how their unique insights can benefit others. Every mistake made, every lesson learned through living, starting, and doing becomes a valuable asset in this introspective journey, offering a fresh perspective on life.

My contribution to this process is driven by a disdain for pointless communication and a passion for meaningful, purposeful exchange. I believe that communication should always serve a purpose; anything less is simply noise. My goal is to guide people in developing a strategy rooted in service. When your work genuinely helps others, appreciation and recognition naturally follow. So, before jumping into any marketing efforts, article writing, or communication plans, it's crucial to ask ourselves: *"How can my knowledge serve others?"* This approach transforms marketing from a barrage of unsolicited messages into a valuable service, offering insights that genuinely help people.

In the method I advocate, professionals are encouraged to:

- Reflect deeply on your identity: **who are you?**
- Gain clarity on your core values: **what do you stand for?**
- Understand who you aim to help: **who do I want to serve?**
- Recognize your expertise and how it can benefit others: **what do I know?**
- Describe the way you can do it: **how can I help others?**
- Sharpen your focus and ensure your contributions are useful: **how can my contribution truly serve them?**

THE "4CS" FORMULA TO INSPIRE AND IMPACT OTHERS

Effective communication is essential for connecting with your ideal clients, community, and collaborators. Helping individuals understand their vision and make it accessible in a clear and engaging manner is invaluable. This is equally important for managers: defining their professional vision, reconstructing their ideas, and then sharing them with a refined language elevates the entire process. This process doesn't mean only improving ourselves; it should also foster a mindset of service, ensuring that every piece of knowledge shared is a gift to those who receive it. A book crafted with this philosophy will live, breathe, and make a significant impact, enhancing the author's journey and offering invaluable insights to the world.

Effective communication hinges on *four crucial pillars*:

1 Clarity: Many people brim with energy and enthusiasm but lack the clarity or opportunity to share their brilliance. Often, our minds are a whirlwind of ideas, making it challenging to articulate thoughts clearly. Articulating a clear message is the foundation.

2 Courage: *"Is anybody else gonna like it? Is it going to make sense? Is it going to be judged? Is it going to be criticized?"* Those are the typical questions that invade our mind. Overcoming the fear of judgment or criticism and daring to share our insights with the world is essential. We need a sufficient amount of courage to be willing to share our vision with others, for other people to see it and hear it, and have access to it.

3 Connection: We don't have to navigate this journey alone. That's not efficient. Collaborating with trusted individuals and leveraging professional insights can streamline the process, avoiding the need to reinvent the wheel. It's amazing how many people can help us move that process along: this collaboration can transform and clarify ideas, making them resonate with others.

4 Consistency: Consistency is the key to mastery. Whether it's writing, consulting, or any other endeavor, practicing diligently enhances our skills and amplifies our impact. By committing to a disciplined and consistent approach, we ensure that our contributions are not only significant but also of the highest quality.

Additionally to this formula there is a continuous and comprehensive process that will transform your vision into a powerful catalyst for change, both within and around you: Reflecting, Re-examining, Re-focusing, and Refining – are then the cornerstones of a transformative journey. Through *reflection*, you gain insight into your true self and your core motivations. *Re-examination* allows you to critically assess your current path and the authenticity of your message. *Re-focusing* sharpens your vision, ensuring it always aligns with your values and goals. Lastly, *refining* your approach and communication ensures that your message not only resonates deeply with your audience but also inspires action, fostering a community united by shared passions and visions. Identifying your vision and sharing it with the world is not just an action; it's a journey. In the era we live in, communication is not just about existing and being found; it's about sharing the most noble parts of ourselves, articulating why you do what you do, the higher purpose of your vision, and thereby fostering a community of passionate followers. Whether you're embarking on a new project or carrying on a legacy, rediscovering and updating the meaning behind your actions is crucial. What is the purpose of our business, our team, now? This purpose might be entirely different from the past, as the world evolves.

Now, leaders, intrapreneurs, and change-makers, is the time to step forward, to embrace the transformative journey of clarifying and spreading your vision. Your vision has the power to ignite a fire of innovation and passion, but it is your responsibility to ensure that this flame never dies out! By turning your vision into an eternal voice, your message will resonate through the ages, inspiring generations to come.

MY TIP FOR A MORE "ETHICAL" BUSINESS: DO EVERYTHING WITH EXCELLENCE AND PRESENCE

Two pillars underpin my values: **excellence** and **presence** with people. This principle has anchored me amidst shifts and transitions, ensuring that every step I take is grounded in quality and mindfulness. In a world where the pace of change is relentless and the competition fierce, adopting a mindset of excellence and presence can set you apart. Whether you're crafting a strategic plan, mentoring a team member, or sharing a meal with your family, *embrace the moment.* Be fully present with your clients, your teams, and your families, with every fiber of your being.

From my transitions in the corporate world to the decision to start my own venture, these values guided my journey. They are influenced by my family, faith, and personal heroes' journey, revealing my capacity to discover and nurture the potential in others. My approach to team management, motivation, and engagement goes beyond tasks; it's about support, creating a profound and extended team, enriching relationships and people. This sense of responsibility – questioning what our responsibility in this new era is – demands and provides not just kindness but a shared commitment to advance together in the new civilization we are creating.

That's the approach that enables me to spend *quality time* with clients who are catalysts for change, driving healthy success within their teams. It's about uncovering the soul of their enterprise and enabling them to share that essence with others and then make meaningful connections that resonate with your core values and vision. I take great pride in spending time with incredibly smart and inspiring individuals. It's a privilege that constantly stimulates growth and learning. I cannot compromise on excellence or presence with the people in my life. My commitment to excellence and being fully present with those I care about – my family, clients, or teams – is unwavering, deeply part of my sense of integrity. This approach ensures that when people are with me, they receive my full attention, heart, and mind. This is what I strive to instill in everyone I work with, ensuring that the noblest parts of ourselves, the precious gems hidden within us, are shared, creating a ripple effect of positive change and inspiration. Through this process, individuals discover who they are, often through writing a book or developing a message, embodying the entrepreneur within. This commitment to presence is what elevates good to great, transforming routine exchanges into moments of true connection and profound impact.

CHALLENGING QUESTIONS

- Consider the essence of your dream or goal. How does it align with your personal values, and how can it contribute to the greater good?
- What practical steps can you take to preserve the integrity and essence of your vision?
- Think about the long-term impact of your potential book. What legacy do you want to leave behind through your words?
- How do your own aspirations in work and life intersect, and what adjustments can you make to ensure they coexist harmoniously?
- In what ways can you embody excellence and presence in your daily life?

ABOUT THE AUTHOR

Denise Cumella is an international bestselling author and the developer of the highly successful BookCamp Method. As the founder and CEO of The Boss Books and Libri d'Impresa Publishing, she helps entrepreneurs and professionals turn their ideas into books and their books into powerful marketing tools. So far, Denise and her team have provided their guidance and support to more than 600 international authors.

Her background includes more than 20 years of experience in marketing and creating high-value content for a variety of companies, such as Lush Cosmetics and Venchi Chocolate. Thanks to her talent and expertise, she has the ability to make customers fall in love with the companies she works with.

The Roots of Acceptance: Uncovering Diversity

Giuseppe Robiati

—

Business consultant with extensive corporate experience. International author, founder at EBBF

"Unity in diversity
is the highest possible
attainment of
a civilization,
a testimony to the most
noble possibilities
of the human race."

Michael Novak

TOLERANCE OR ACCEPTANCE?

In a world increasingly interconnected, ethical business practices are essential. They offer a way forward in a landscape marred by inequality and exploitation, creating a future where prosperity is shared and diversity is celebrated. But how do you do this? By embracing and managing *diversity* – not just in terms of race or gender but also in religion, problem-solving approaches, age, and life experiences. This deep **understanding and acceptance of diversity** goes beyond tolerance; it is a profound sharing of life's diverse realities.

"We are all leaves of the same tree"

Many years ago, I led a large multinational company with numerous facilities facing a personnel shortage. We needed to begin hiring individuals who were not from the typical Northern Italian cultural background, characterized by being white, male, and Catholic. After much discussion and deliberation, we decided to hire the first 50 people from North Africa. Upon their arrival, we conducted a brief orientation on key work-related terms, safety procedures, and essential daily tasks before they commenced their jobs. However, a month later, they went on strike, prompting us to visit their facility to understand the cause. It turned out that the company's canteen was not equipped to cater to Muslim dietary requirements, failing to provide suitable meal options. Consequently, we revised the canteen menus to include options that accommodated their *needs.*

After some time, the Italian staff went on strike, citing that the African employees worked less due to their thrice-daily prayer sessions in the factory square, which resulted in them working an hour and a half less each day. This led to perceptions of *unfairness* among the Italian workers. In response, we convened a meeting to address the issue of diversity acceptance and proposed a solution where the North African employees could compensate for the lost hours by working on Saturdays. This proposal was accepted, allowing us to move forward.

As the company grew, we encountered the need to hire individuals from regions other than North Africa. We then recruited Indian workers, who, unlike the Muslims from North Africa, had different dietary needs due to their Buddhist or Hindu faiths, often practicing vegetarianism. So we had to reorganize the whole system, giving all groups the possibility of having their own diversity of life. Gradually, an understanding and respect for diversity deepened. I later organized a conference to elucidate the concept of diversity, likening it to the varied leaves of a tree that, despite their differences, are all integral parts of the same entity. A month after this conference, I received an African Ficus in my office with a note stating, *"We are all leaves of the same tree"* affirming that the concept of diversity had been wholeheartedly embraced within my company.

A TREE WITHOUT STRONG ROOTS DRIES UP: ACCEPTING THE FIVE DIMENSIONS OF DIVERSITY

We are unique individuals in the universe; everyone we encounter differs from us, necessitating the acceptance of each other's differences. But how exactly does the system for fostering diversity acceptance operate on a conceptual level? Achieving acceptance demands **profound understanding**, organized into *five levels of* *acceptance*, which are essential for ethical business practices and work relationships. Each of these levels can be developed and enhanced through targeted training and improvement efforts:

1. Physical acceptance: *accepting visible differences*
This encompasses embracing variances in gender, origin, religion, knowledge, lifestyle, attire, and diet. If we remain on this – more superficial – level, we have lost the game as this pertains solely to work activities manifested through the physical body. To prevent stagnation, it's imperative to enrich this level, thereby urging individuals to pursue education on sustaining a healthy physical state, such as participating in nutrition and healthy lifestyle courses.

2. Knowledge and competencies: *the wisdom of assessing and* valuing competencies
Assessing and valuing competencies necessitates evaluators who possess the requisite skills for fair judgment. This second level thrives on training aimed at enhancing existing skills and acquiring new ones, essential in an ever-evolving world. It's crucial to adapt and align our capabilities with the continuously expanding landscape of competencies, ensuring we remain competitive and effective in our respective fields. This dynamic approach to skill development not only enriches individual prowess but also fortifies the collective proficiency within an organization.
In today's society, acceptance of individuals is predominantly grounded in the initial two aspects mentioned. However, additional layers of acceptance have gained significant importance over the past fifty years, yet they frequently go unrecognized. To foster a more inclusive and comprehensive environment, it's imperative to

integrate these subsequent levels of acceptance into our business interactions with those around us, including our supervisors, employees, and colleagues. These dimensions contribute to a richer understanding and more meaningful connections within the workplace, enhancing collaboration and mutual respect.

3. Emotional level: *sharing your why*

Recognizing that emotions can affect work quality and relationships is key. It is crucial to learn to manage emotions by sharing the reasons behind our feelings and creating opportunities for open consultation. The emotional level is often overlooked because it is believed not to produce business value according to most of today's entrepreneurs. However, if neglected, it can indeed decrease value. For example, if someone arrives at work on Monday morning, angry and frustrated due to personal issues, these emotions can lead to poor work quality, strained relationships with others, and a deteriorating relationship with their employer and the ongoing business. If an individual faces challenges at home, such as a drug-addicted child or separation from their spouse, these emotions can *lower physical efficiency* and competencies, impacting the quality of these two first elements.

Emotions are like bells; if I start ringing my bell, someone else hears my bell and thinks, "Ah, we can ring the bell," they ring it too, and by the evening, an equivalent number of bells to those of St. Peter's Basilica ring, adversely affecting the company. *Decisions should never be made at the peak of emotional states*, as such decisions are fundamentally flawed. Emotions have the potential to weaken and dissolve relationships with others or to generate conflicts because they can hardly be controlled on the moment itself. If everyone gives free rein to their emotions, then emotions must be moderated through sharing. Explaining the reasons behind our feelings helps to dissipate them and reduces focus on the behavior itself.

4. Willpower: nourishing with encouragement rather than judgment. The fourth level of acceptance involves the domain of willpower. Willpower is the force each of us requires to attain a result, reach a goal, to prove ourselves that we can make it, and drive towards a specific achievement. We are not used to considering the role of willpower in individuals because it needs to be nurtured with a kind of food that is scarcely utilized in contemporary society – this nourishment is *encouragement*. Many of us may not have received adequate encouragement in our familial environments, academic endeavors, or professional life, whether as employees or entrepreneurs, due to the prevalence of judgment. Encouragement is the catalyst that unlocks the concealed inner energy necessary for realizing objectives. It transcends the mere allocation of financial rewards to employees, instead focusing on recognizing the excellence of their contributions. A piece of advice: the most effective form of encouragement is public acknowledgment, which highlights and celebrates often overlooked merits.

5. Inner qualities: when our soul comes into play.
The fifth level represents the realm of inner qualities, often referred to as the value or spiritual level. In this context, "spiritual" doesn't pertain to religious affiliation but rather to the inherent forces within us that come to the forefront during challenging times. In today's world, it's no longer sufficient for a personnel manager to conduct interviews solely based on personal likability and competencies.

There exists a critical dimension of values that has to be taken into consideration. For instance, consider an administrative director with impeccable competencies evident from their curriculum and financial acumen. While technical prowess is vital, questions about their values are equally crucial. Do they exhibit transparency in budgeting? Are they truthful in their communications and when faced with budgetary challenges that require ethical decisions? These questions delve into the realm of trust, which hinges on one's values. Similarly, a sales manager role responsible for negotiating customer orders involves concerns about potential corruption or behaviors that might undermine the company's interests. CEOs, who wield significant power, face complex challenges in wielding that power responsibly. Discriminatory behavior, gender bias, and internal conflicts are also some of the pitfalls of mismanaged power within companies.

The spectrum of inner qualities is vast. Some indispensable qualities for effective human relationships, particularly in a business context, encompass *sincerity, transparency, courage, resilience, patience, and a wholehearted acceptance of diversity.* When we access this fifth level world, there is a profound acceptance of all the diversities of the previous four levels.

The sweet fruit of ethical business

Failure to harmonize and integrate these five levels can undoubtedly give rise to conflicts and disputes, which are business destroyers. These dimensions form the bedrock of ethical business practices, as they foster the holistic development of individuals, extending beyond their roles as employees. They are the very essence of personal and organizational prosperity. If we were to visualize these five levels, they would resemble a tree, with the fifth level serving as its roots. Just as a *tree* with strong roots thrives and grows, *a business that nurtures these five levels can truly flourish.* A tree without strong roots dries up, does not grow, and dies. That's why the value part must be strong and developed through the acquisition of knowledge of these values. The fourth level where courage and will are, is the level of breaking the prejudices around us. So when the sprout of the plant breaks the soil and emerges into the open, the courage to demonstrate one's worth becomes the opening of the roots to the earth, giving rise to what will be the future trunk. Following this, we have the emotional and intellectual facets, symbolizing the branches and flowers, while the physical level, in this context, represents the ultimate fruition of all these efforts – the fruit itself. A tree with strong roots and a nurtured structure yields sweet fruit – the productive, appreciated, and desired outcomes of an ethical business.

Let me share another story with you. We had a factory in Tuscany where the director, a young engineer, was reported to be wandering all day with his phone, endangering his safety inside the factory. Research was conducted, and it was discovered that he was on the phone all day with his wife, who was in the hospital because she had just given birth, and there were some complications with the baby. Therefore, this young man's emotions were sky-high. So I called him and said, "Stefano, I know what your problem is. Starting from Monday morning, you stop working. You will be paid, but you will spend your time in the hospital with your wife, and this is an order that cannot be refused." A month passed, and one day my assistant told me, "Stefano's wife came to Milan and wants to speak with you." – Eh, Stefano's wife came from Tuscany to speak to me, what's up, what's there? – She comes in, crying, and says, "Engineer, I came to thank you because without the presence of my husband, we would not have solved the problem."

What happened? She felt protected, he felt *protected*, he felt *understood*. He realized that his emotions went beyond the level of guarding, and we assisted him in successfully executing a comprehensive operation that included the active involvement in his family life.

In recent times, we've had various experiences, one notable example being our initiative to bring employees' families into the factories where their fathers work. A particularly heartwarming experience took place in Turin, at a factory specializing in agricultural machinery exported worldwide. Here, we welcomed the wives and children of our employees. The children, having studied environmental issues in school, were delighted to learn that their fathers were contributing to a market that produced environmentally-friendly machinery. This fostered a profound connection between families and the company, with everyone feeling proud to have a father employed in such a forward-thinking factory. It underscores the importance of involving families in a company's ethical activities, as it enriches the bonds between employees, their families, and the organization.

THE TRANSFORMATION: FROM PYRAMID TO DAISY

Comparing the company before and after these principles were applied, we saw a transformation. Initially, the focus was solely on physical appearance and competencies, but as we began to address and integrate the other levels, the culture shifted. We moved from a hierarchical pyramid model to a 'Daisy Management' model, with departments like petals around a central executive team. Decision-making became more inclusive, quicker, and less conflict-ridden.

The management of power can no longer be at an individual level. It must be brought to a level of *sharing*. No decision can be made alone; it must be made in a group. Each individual, like a finger of a hand, has a power, each individual has a strength, but the true strength is the *unity* of the employees through collaboration.

The Daisy Management means that individual power is deconstructed. The organizational chart is like a daisy: the executive team is at the center coordinating the work of all the departments, which are the petals. Today, we have to go beyond the hierarchical single-mind system and transform all business operations in a pluri-minded system where there is no longer a singular boss, but rather people are in contact with the system and with each other.

As a consultant, I'm currently engaged with numerous companies in establishing a management structure that avoids personal power in favor of shared decision-making power. This board comprises individuals from within the company as well as external experts. The goal is to shift from a centralized, single-minded approach ("Uniminded") to one that embraces shared authority ("Pluriminded"). This approach facilitates swifter, more harmonious decision-making processes that minimize conflicts.

A TIP FOR YOU: Keep learning!

How can you see this transformation in your company? Entrepreneurs and managers need to conduct managerial training courses on accepting diversities because you cannot learn these things on your own; hence, you must have activities in which people learn among their peers.

Training should not be perceived as a cost; it's a strategic investment. In today's context, it's imperative for effective people management. Just as engineers undergo training to plan programs, individuals should also consider courses on managing people and creating conducive environments for their growth and success. In the modern world, you can possess cutting-edge technology, machinery, and advanced AI programs, but without skilled individuals, effective management remains elusive.

It's fundamental to conduct managerial training programs that provide ongoing opportunities for individuals to learn how to manage people effectively. Even in a landscape filled with computers, machines, and AI, the human element remains indispensable. The key is to ensure that people are placed in the right conditions to thrive and contribute to organizational success.

ABOUT THE AUTHOR

Giuseppe Robiati, co-founder of EBBF in 1990, has been an industrial manager and CEO of Scac Group, a large company with 14 facilities in Italy, Brazil, Argentina, Canada, and Albania. Now he uses his experience to help companies move towards shared growth and sharing.

Where is the Best version of Yourself Hiding?

Martina Crepaz

—

Health coach & digital marketing consultant

*"Fortify yourself
with moderation;
for this is an
impregnable
fortress."*

Epictetus

THE BEST VERSION OF YOURSELF PART ONE: HEALTH AND MODERATION

I help people become the best version of themselves, by facilitating their wellbeing transformation.

Why does this matter so much to me?

Because I truly believe that a change in your health can have both a positive impact on your job, on your personal relationships and on the way you finally impact the world. You may want to change something in your life but you are stuck and you don't know how to make that change. Most probably you are procrastinating, and you have been doing so for a very long time. Maybe it is just a question of lack of self-confidence, or a matter of acceptance. In my opinion, I think we must all start reconsidering the concept of self-acceptance.

I believe that, in order to build a better future, we should start accepting diversity. I don't mean just accepting it, but embracing it. First of all, this process must start by accepting our own diversity. The diversity of our way of looking and being, who we are and how we perceive ourselves being.

Within this frame, my priority is to talk about **health** because I think there is a big misconception about it; health doesn't only regard "diseases and illnesses", health and wellness is strongly linked to all aspects of our lives and in many cases involves a lack of moderation.

Too much of anything is never healthy.

Too little of anything is never healthy.

When all things are enjoyed in moderation, it empowers you to prioritize the cultivation of your well-being and happiness, fostering sustainable transformation. Consistently nurturing healthy habits over extended periods of time, can result in easing or reversing symptoms of poor health as well as support other areas in your life that might be needing your attention.

THE BEST VERSION OF YOURSELF PART TWO: PRIORITIZE YOUR LIFE AND BUILD A COMMUNITY

You may feel lost, alone, but I'm going to show you that the second or third or even a fourth life is possible. You're not going through this journey of transformation alone. Change is always positive and it's something you can achieve if you fight with strength, motivation and commitment. Also, setting aside pride and seeking assistance are vital steps in this transformative process.

In my consulting practice, I strive to help people become the best version of themselves by connecting people and connecting expertise.

Our aim when assisting others is not to simply hand them pre-packaged solutions, but rather to empower them in discovering their own paths to resolution. Each individual's journey is unique, and the solutions that resonate most deeply are those tailored to their specific needs, eliminating barriers along the way. What might appear daunting to one person could be trivial to another, highlighting the importance of personalized support and understanding from both perspectives.

My team but above all my clients are committed and really, really want to change, but they just don't know how to do it. We want to build communities helping each other to solve problems, empower and elevate one another and we want to be that connection, the missing dot. We aim to bridge gaps and simplify complexities, all with the ultimate goal of guiding people towards their fullest potential. Our empathy stems from firsthand experience: we've walked similar paths and truly understand the challenges.

That giant sense of procrastination, lack of self-confidence and self-love, can be overcome by creating a safe space, by exploring and experimenting a new self or an old self that is coming back to life.

THE BEST VERSION OF YOURSELF PART THREE: BELIEVE IN THE POWER OF FREEDOM

We fully appreciate and praise the value of freedom. The freedom of being yourself; the freedom of being whatever you want; the freedom to become whoever you feel you are. You will find appreciation; you will find a family and a community; you will achieve that feeling of belonging that you have probably been missing for a long time.

Think about it in an honest way, if not you, who can do it? And if not now, when will you do it?

If you lack commitment, if you lack self-love or if you spend your time procrastinating probably it is not the right time yet for you to embark on a transformational journey. But, if you respect yourself, if you accept yourself then you already made the first step and together we are going to co-create your new life, your new best version of yourself.

Let me share with you a story. For many, many years I used to think that my worthiness was influenced directly by what and how much I was producing. I had to produce as much as I could in the least possible time. There was no time for healthy food, no time for physical activity, or introspection about who I was and wanted to be. Just even simply think how my day went, how I interacted with my colleagues, my boss, my family, my friends. The famous so called **"Work-life balance" didn't exist at all**.

Until I decided to **prioritize** myself, I started to exercise to embrace the diversity of my body. I started following a healthier diet, in order to nurture both my physical and mental well-being. Incorporating yoga, meditation, and moments of gratitude into my daily routine became non-negotiable.

When I started practicing a healthier routine, I also started seeing that feeling better with myself had a positive impact on on my relationships and professional endeavors. It started influencing the quality of my work, my efficiency and productivity. What before took me a full day to do, now suddenly I could do it in a third of the time, because I was prioritizing something else, I was prioritizing my well-being.

But I easily and quickly got to the point where my relationship with my own health was not moderated. I actually realized I was not truly embracing the diversity of my body. My pursuit of health and perfection converted into an unhealthy obsession. Despite appearing outwardly strong and fit, internally, I struggled to accept my body's diversity. I fixated on food and exercise to an unsustainable extent, sacrificing sleep and peace of mind in the process.

This was not a balanced and healthy lifestyle. So, I did stop and embarked on a period of self-reflection. I sought balance and moderation, embracing my body and its unique qualities. As a good connector, with the support of a dedicated network of health professionals, I crafted a new routine aligned with my values and aspirations. Together, we navigated the complexities of self-acceptance and holistic well-being, forming a cohesive team dedicated to personal growth and fulfillment.

When you work with me, I will support and accompany you in transforming your well-being to a sustainable extent so that you can become the best version of yourself by facilitating the connection to the right expert you need in your life in order to look and feel who you want to be. You will not be alone in this journey because I believe in the power of love, of unity, of connection.

I believe in the **power of network**.

IN SUMMARY

This message is for all the Martinas out there. For those who really want to change, who really want to become the best version of themselves but don't know from where to start. For those that are probably unstructured and not organized and need the right person to guide them through their change. This is for those who touch the bottom but are ready to reach the light again, and for those who need support and encouragement to believe in themselves and unlock their full potential.

I'm really aiming to help people become the the most authentic and fulfilled version of themselves and live the best chapters of their lives that are yet to unfold. My joy and compensation comes from seeing happy, fulfilled people; I gain joy by facilitating other people's lives and simplifying the intricate complexities that may be hindering their paths to self-realization.

My ultimate piece of advice is to be kind to yourself. Sometimes you are not ready for that change and you must accept it. Learn how to recognize the right moment, and wait for it. Wait for the moment when you feel you are strong enough to make the first step. Once you feel the moment has arrived, go for it!

Because nobody is going to do that change for you. If not now, then when will you take the reins of your own transformation and pursue it wholeheartedly?

CHALLENGING QUESTIONS

- Have you ever visualized your future self? (Think about your whole and perfect self in one, five or even ten years from now)
- What are your goals and vision? And, how would you like to tackle them? Do you need support with this process?.
- Have you ever viewed yourself from the lens of self-compassion and love?
- Do you self-sabotage with fear of failure thoughts?
- Are you a procrastinator or are you one who doesn't know how to hit the pause button?
- Are you trying to always please others at the risk of burnout?
- Do you criticize, judge others including yourself?

ABOUT THE AUTHOR

Martina Crepaz is a highly skilled mentor and community builder, passionate about guiding individuals toward their best selves. With over 15 years of experience, she has successfully coached numerous international individuals and teams on their personal development journeys. Her coaching maturity is highlighted by her professional accomplishments and a deep understanding of diverse cultures. This is further enriched by her exceptional project management skills and her personal journey of transformation while living and working in various countries.

Pascal Jossi

The Hard Truth About Soft Skills

Pascal Jossi

—

Facilitator and Corporate Culture Consultant

"The degree to which
I can create relationships,
which facilitate the growth
of others as separate
persons, is a measure
of the growth
I have achieved in myself."

Carl Rogers

THE RIPPLE EFFECT OF ETHICAL BUSINESSES

In my view, an *ethical business* is one that cultivates prosperity for everyone.

The governance model of such a business is human-centric and its main purpose should be creating an environment where every individual, from the janitor to the CEO, can flourish.

It's only in such a setting that a constructive work culture can emerge and bring tangible impact on its members, steering them towards their best selves. The effect of such a nurturing environment doesn't just stop at the office doors. It's when employees are encouraged to grow and excel, that they can carry these qualities into other areas of their lives – families, friendships, and community engagements. Thus, a company's empowering culture extends its influence far beyond its walls. That's how a thriving internal community can become a powerful force for societal good.

As we can see, being an ethical business clearly transcends internal culture. It must also positively influence its surrounding community, including customers, suppliers, public authorities, and the environment. True ethical status is achieved when a business is driven by a purpose greater than profit and when all stakeholders benefit from its operations. This creates a synergistic win-win situation for everyone involved.

But a word of caution is needed at this point: when it comes to transforming an organization into a force for good, the devil is in the details. Building a positive work culture is actually a nuanced process.

While decisions on overarching strategies and business models are important, the real game is played by smaller "less significant" interactions. Let me give you some examples to illustrate this idea.

WHEN GOOD INTENTIONS MEET TOUGH REALITIES

Many don't know that my professional journey began in the classroom, where I, like many educators, worked to create a safe and nurturing environment favorable for learning. As teachers, we learn to juggle numerous relationships and dynamics among students – while carefully moderating our own emotions to avoid being provoked by challenging behavior.

You would expect these qualities to translate seamlessly into creating a harmonious work environment among colleagues. Yet, when it came to collaborative projects like organizing the end of the year festival, I witnessed surprisingly the opposite: tension would mount, discussions would become heated and the loudest most assertive group would impose their will and eclipse other voices. The result? A general sense of frustration coupled with disengagement. The burden of implementation weighed heavily on the shoulders of a few, while the silent majority felt overlooked and disconnected from projects, they had no interest in.

Flashforward a few years, as an independent facilitator and community builder, I witnessed a similar scenario in a different setting: a financial company I was working with, aimed to foster a positive work culture. The CEO therefore organized weekly lunch gatherings to have an open dialogue about the state of the company.

This noble and initially celebrated initiative, devolved slowly into a venting session. The outcome? Again, general frustration! The CEO grew defensive in the face of blunt criticism, while employees felt ignored because their concerns stayed seemingly unaddressed.

These experiences are clearly tied together by a recurring phenomenon that manifests in many organizations: even with best intentions and the most welcoming spaces for collaboration, the outcome is still tensions and disengagement. Why? Should setting the right frame not be enough for people to engage with one another in a meaningful way?

Well, from an educational perspective, from primary school to university, our journey was largely individualistic. We learned to excel in our personal academic pursuits but we were rarely thought on how to navigate the complexities of group dynamics. In my experience, even when group assignments arose, we were given topics but mostly left alone and without guidance on the human aspect of project management. So, in terms of process, we had similar results as I would later witness as teacher: a few that lead, assign tasks, and the rest contribute in isolation – if at all. A coincidence? I don't think so. In my view it's simply the logical consequence; when it comes to collaboration, many people enter the workforce totally unprepared and then replicate unconsciously old patterns.

To bridge this gap, many organizations invest massive amounts of resources into soft skill training without getting the desired results. Unfortunately, it is still often overseen that the effectiveness of such training is correlated to our understanding of what soft skills truly entail.

THE HARD TRUTH ABOUT SOFT SKILLS

Soft skills are often misunderstood. To get a clearer picture of the misconceptions surrounding soft skills we have to dissect the term into its two components **"Soft"** and **"Skill"**.

1) From soft to essential

Generally speaking, the term "soft skills" evokes an image of **non-critical** perhaps even weak. In many organizations they are viewed as a supplement to the hard skills, a luxury afforded only when the targets of business performance are met – basically a **nice-to-have**, but not essential. This is where the misconception begins and, unfortunately, where the potential of an organization starts to be undermined.

The prevalent *'get the job done'* mentality in many work cultures glorifies hitting targets and prioritizes outcomes over processes. It's an approach that measures your contributions and value almost exclusively through the prism of financial gain. This short-sighted approach totally neglects the broader, more holistic view of organizational health and growth. For instance, in law firms, a partner's (manager) worth is often reduced to the volume of new clients brought in during a year. Other contributions, such as investing time in training associates (juniors), are undervalued because they don't directly correlate with immediate profitability. However, if we pause to examine the longer-term impact, the benefits of so-called *soft skills* become evident. A partner who nurtures a well-trained, cohesive team, creates the conditions for a high performing team. This, in turn, can lead to **higher client satisfaction, a stronger firm reputation**, and **reduced costs** through lower staff turnover. It goes even further, ironically, the very neglect of soft skills in pursuit of immediate results can lead to a decline in the metrics that the 'get the job done' mentality prizes. A **lack of trust** or mounting frustration can lead to **lower work engagement**. This **collective underperformance** inevitably impacts **client retention**, leading to **reduced revenue** and a company operating in a **constant state of crisis**. Suddenly, the 'softness' of these skills doesn't seem so soft after all.

The reality is that *soft skills* such communication, listening, teamwork and leadership are critical to the success of any enterprise. They are not just complementary; they are **essential**.

2) From skills to capabilities

To address the second common misconception surrounding 'soft skills,' we must first understand how they relate to capabilities.

Capabilities are the comprehensive abilities that enable us to perform complex tasks effectively. According to the transformative leadership framework, they're not standalone traits but formed through the interdependent development of 4 elements: knowledge, skills, attitudes, and qualities.

- **Knowledge:** To acquire a new *capability*, one must grasp its underlying concepts and theories. This knowledge forms the foundation for later practical application. For instance, developing the capability for effective meetings necessitates learning about focus, attention span, decision-making processes, and non-violent communication, among other things.
- **Attitudes:** This refers to the emotional and psychological stances we adopt, such as a willingness to learn, openness to new ideas, tolerance of ambiguity, and a spirit of curiosity.

These attitudes shape how we approach our work and interactions.

- **Qualities:** They represent the ideal human behavior. Think of qualities such as honesty, reliability, integrity.
- **Skills:** Finally, skills represent the functional and mechanical abilities that allow a person to execute a capability. These are your hands-on tools, the actual techniques you use to get things done. In the context of leading meetings for instance, this includes creating agendas, taking notes, and summarizing outcomes effectively.

By using this quadrant of elements, we see that what we call, generally speaking, *a soft skill* may indeed be a part of a *capability* or, in some cases, a *capability* itself. This distinction or **shift in perspective** can be a **crucial game changer**. How? By identifying whether a soft skill is a standalone capability or an aspect of a larger one, we can tailor our approach to learning and growth. For example, let's take a look at effective communication. At first it might seem like a singular skill, but in reality it encapsulates knowledge of language nuances, the attitude of openness, the quality of clarity, and the skill of articulation. Recognizing these components enables us to dissect and enhance each one, thus strengthening the overall *capability.*

Conversely, if we understand that what we've been calling a *soft skill* is actually for example an attitude, such as curiosity, we can then look for the overarching capability that we actually want to develop. This gives us again the possibility to identify related knowledge, qualities, and skills.

This **paradigm shift** from *soft skill* to *capability* is more than semantic, it allows us to better connect the dots and fill in the gaps. It opens the potential for a more well-rounded development of the capabilities that are pivotal to the success of our endeavors.

Shifting our understanding of soft skills to essential capabilities naturally transforms our **approach to training**. Traditional training methods in organizations often focus on upskilling or expanding the knowledge of team members. This form of *informative learning* which adds new facts, concepts, and skills to our repertoire is valuable and has its merits.

For example, we all sit more comfortable in a plane, when we know that the pilot navigating our flight has undergone extensive training and possesses a wealth of experience. But in the bigger picture, this conventional approach represents only a portion of the developmental journey. It enriches our knowledge base of a topic but often fails to alter our fundamental perceptions. Taking again the example of our pilot, his extensive informative learning journey, does not automatically qualify him to be a good leader for his aircrew.

True capability building requires a more holistic method: *transformative learning*. This approach goes beyond mere information acquisition; it catalyzes a **profound shift** in our worldviews and mental models. *Transformative learning* is not just about absorbing new techniques or strategies, it integrates also attitudes and qualities, thus embracing the full spectrum of human experience. When we engage in transformative learning, we challenge and change our very way of thinking, leading to **personal and professional evolution**.

This type of learning demands that we bring our whole selves to the process, questioning our preconceived notions and opening ourselves to new, sometimes uncomfortable, insights. In a nutshell, during this learning process, we allow ourselves to re-configurate our frame of reference to accommodate and leverage novel ideas and perspectives.

When organizations create the right conditions and invest in *transformative learning*, they receive more than upskilled employees, they nurture **agents of change**. These transformed individuals not only equip their teams with essential capabilities but also empower them with a reinvigorated **sense of purpose**. Each member's personal growth contributes to the **collective success** and to a **positive work culture**, ensuring the organization is not just enduring but dynamically evolving in today's fast-paced world.

So how can organizations leverage transformative learning-?

- When crafting a capability-building plan, whether for yourself or your organization, prioritize transformative learning experiences that encompass all four elements: concepts, skills, attitudes, and qualities. Also opt for programs that challenge and extend you or your colleagues comfort zone. Over time, make transformative learning your new standard, not an exception. Getting used to transformative learning will help you and your team become better leaders as you will no longer be afraid of uncomfortable situations but see them as opportunities for individual and collective growth.

- For organizations, it's imperative to cultivate a post-learning environment where new capabilities can be applied in practice, not just in theory. This hands-on application is what cements learning and prevents a regression to old patterns. Capabilities thrive best in action.
- One reason why we like to stick with only skills and concepts in capability building framework, is because they are measurable. There are easy ways to find out if somebody mastered a method or is more knowledgeable about a topic. Measuring the intangible on the other side, like an increase in compassion or open-mindedness, may seem challenging, but it's a crucial aspect of capability building. We have to move beyond traditional metrics and engage in regular qualitative methods like, meaningful conversations, mindful interviews, and reflective self-assessments. To identify progress enough time between these evaluations is needed; the components of capabilities often don't evolve linearly or in parallel. For instance, there may be a need for an initial focus on knowledge to lay the groundwork for subsequent skill and attitude development. Or sometimes a transformative experience might first change our attitude before we even understand the underlying concepts.

Ultimately, the goal is to foster an environment where **continuous capability growth** is nurtured, valued, and visible. Unlike to the more rigid soft-skill approach, *capability building* equips team members with the flexibility to adapt to novel scenarios and offers a framework to constructively navigate the subtle challenges that shape our work culture. By choosing *this transformative learning approach* we not just build a skilled workforce but a collective of **change makers**, ready to contribute to the success and ethical evolution of the organization.

CHALLENGING QUESTIONS

- What are the key capabilities you believe are essential for fostering an ethical work environment in your organization?
- Now think in terms of knowledge, skills, attitudes, and qualities. How do you plan to develop these capabilities for yourself and others encompassing these four levels?
- What initiatives or programs can you introduce to promote a culture of continuous capability growth in your organization?
- What strategies can you implement to facilitate transformative learning within your organization, ensuring it leads to meaningful personal and professional growth for all employees?
- What practical steps can you take to ensure that the capabilities developed through transformative learning are actively applied and integrated into the daily operations and decision-making processes of your organization?

ABOUT THE AUTHOR

Pascal Jossi is a facilitator and corporate culture consultant with a solid foundation in education, labor sciences and leadership. He brings several years of project management experience, particularly in long-term capacity-development and community building projects. In his current role, he specializes in facilitating trainings and workshops aimed at assisting companies in their journey to build capabilities and transform their organizations into communities. Moreover, he mentors aspiring facilitators, empowering them to excel in their roles. Driven by the belief that the future of work lies in purpose-driven collaboration, he is dedicated to pioneering new ways of working that align with the evolving demands of the 21st century.

It's Time to Reinvent the Concept of Success

Mónica Martínez Vargas

—

Executive Director | Business & Leadership Consultant | C level Coach | Leading Regenerative Projects | Mentor of young talents | Advisory board member ebbf | At the SERVICE of the UNITY of MANKIND | ♥

"None of us, including me, ever do great things. But we can all do small things, with great love, and together we can do something wonderful."

Mother Theresa

In these unprecedented times, when all paradigms are falling apart, many people are working alone, with a silo mentality, without having the opportunity to share any goals or values with their coworkers. This is affecting both companies and individuals, leading to a general lack of motivation and mass resignation.

This situation can be partly attributed to the nature of the key performance indicators that companies use to evaluate the achievements of their employees. KPIs often force individuals to work on their own rather than in teams, and to accomplish their objectives irrespective of what other colleagues or departments are doing. People are encouraged to compete instead of collaborating, which inevitably leads to a silo mentality and a total lack of synergy within the company.

When management doesn't promote collaboration, different departments end up competing for resources, adopting an "us against them" mentality, and there is a breakdown in internal communication. This lack of unity in the organizational culture creates an unhealthy work environment and prevents people from focusing on the big picture.

But how can a company thrive and achieve lasting success with this type of mindset? A business that fosters short-termism and competition is bound to pay less attention to strategy and long-term value creation for both the company and its people.

Unity and synergy are crucial in any business environment. It's essential for any business to understand and emphasize the power of collaboration, empathy and trust. Through unity and collaboration, we can accomplish much more than we could ever do on our own. It is only by breaking out of our silos and creating relationships with a meaningful purpose that we can build sustainable ecosystems based on trust, collaboration and love.

It's time for companies to reinvent performance indicators and give a new meaning to the concept of success. How can this be achieved? There are two main ways to bring lasting change to your company culture:

- Focusing on nourishing people
- Promoting collaboration instead of competition, thus breaking out of the silo mentality and shifting your focus from personal success to team achievement.

COLLABORATION AS THE KEY TO A MORE SUSTAINABLE WORK ENVIRONMENT

I work with executives and managers operating in a variety of sectors to help them find a more sustainable way to do business. My clients include government organizations, international engineering companies, mining companies and family businesses. They ask for my support because they need new tools, techniques and methodologies that will bring them together and lead them to collaborate, innovate and work as one team. My role is to give them the right tools to create alignment and achieve happiness and results, while also providing spaces for hope, balance and spirituality.

They come to me because they feel isolated, disconnected and generally uncomfortable with a work environment characterized by very little trust and a low level of collaboration. CEOs often feel lonely because they don't have anybody to discuss their ideas with, while managers find it difficult to cope with the amount of pressure they have to endure. Because of their position within the company, they are expected to have all the answers and are not allowed to show any weakness, doubt or vulnerability in the workplace. Most of them are workaholics and focus all their physical and mental energies on achieving the best results for their companies. As a consequence, they are constantly stressed out and in serious danger of burning out.

They realize that their lifestyle has become unsustainable, but they just don't know how to change it, because they're unaware of any other options. Since they've always worked that way and they see everybody else doing the same, they cannot imagine a different approach. Therefore, my first task is to open their eyes to the possibility of changing all this. I show them that there is a way to do it and guide them through a transformation process that enables them to be themselves, connect with their mission in life, bring out their talents, and find meaning in their work by serving others.

I help them create safe spaces where we can learn together, listen to each other and collaborate to develop new, healthier approaches that will benefit them, their company and ultimately our society. We focus on a variety of issues, such as how to share their knowledge, how to develop a collaborative attitude in the workplace, and how to give more autonomy to their collaborators. It's important for all team members to be involved in the process, so they can be part of the transformation. If they can work in an environment that fosters trust, autonomy and collaboration, they will be much more motivated and able to contribute their ideas. This new attitude will benefit both the company and the workers themselves, leading the team and the whole organization to success.

In my personal experience, I've seen some amazing results in group settings. A few hours of work on these topics are enough for them to see and appreciate the benefits of this change in mindset. Once they become aware of the possibilities, they are willing to go the extra mile to collaborate and build community in the workplace, because they understand how important it is to support each other and grow together.

GROWING BY SERVING OTHERS

Personal and professional growth is another key factor in this transformation. By collaborating and sharing ideas with our coworkers, we can learn and grow much more than we do when pursuing our separate goals. Our lives become much more balanced, because we start working on ourselves, venturing outside our comfort zone, and developing our integrated selves in a holistic way. The relationships we create will bring extra value not only to us as individuals, but also to our family, friends, coworkers, company, and community.

To achieve real growth, though, it's essential to focus on serving others. You need to ask yourself: "How can I put all my talents at the service of others?" This is a very important piece in the transformational process, because it's what will give real purpose and meaning to your life. You will achieve real fulfillment only if you engage in meaningful activities, making big or small changes to serve your own community or other communities.

Here are a few practical tips that can help you reach this goal:

- Overcome the feeling of isolation by sharing your problems and ideas and encouraging others to do the same. This creates empathy.
- Adopt a positive attitude, be open and vulnerable. This creates trust.
- Ask yourself the following question: "What capacities should I develop to make my team flourish?"
- Look at the bigger picture and ask yourself: "How can I use my talents to serve humanity?" You will grow and achieve real fulfillment by serving others.

Everything becomes easier if you collaborate with others and connect with your purpose in life: this change in attitude will give new meaning to your relationships, to your work and to every moment of your day. It will be a powerful catalyst for transformational results in your professional and personal life.

This different mindset can enlighten the world. When we start listening to each other, we open our hearts and change the vocabulary we use in business. We act differently, build trust and move from fear to love – bringing love and unity into our organizations is the only way forward.

CHALLENGING QUESTIONS

- How balanced is your life?
- How do you measure success in your personal and professional life?
- How can you contribute to creating unity and collaboration in your workplace?
- How can you put your talents at the service of others?

ABOUT THE AUTHOR

Mónica Martínez Vargas is a Chemical Engineer with 30+ years of professional experience who graduated with an MBA with honors from Regis University in Colorado, USA, focused on International Business Development. She is certified as a Project Manager at the University of Denver and is certified as an international coach and facilitator. Mónica is currently Director of ebbf Hispan@s and an advisory member of the global Board of ebbf: Ethical Business Building the future, she is a member of GCBL; Global Chamber of Business Leaders representing Chile, she is a member of the innovation and technology council for the US embassy and is Director of Strategy 2 Succeed in the Consulting and Leadership sector at a global level, with a systemic and strategic approach for the growth of its clients. She leads serving multinational clients in the field of mining, engineering and project construction. During this time, Mónica has specialized in the development, implementation and promotion of transformation programs that allow leaders and their companies to reach higher levels of maturity and consciousness. She leads with confidence and respect, aimed at impacting people's quality of life and achieving her clients' goals. Innovative, creative, and passionate. Among her most outstanding talents we can affirm that Mónica successfully manages intellectual capital; she promotes talent retention; she becomes an agent of organizational change; promotes collaborative learning; regenerative listening, collaboration, expansion of consciousness and quality of life; expands the scope of action of people and work teams; she implements structural, functional, and social transformations.

Bruno Monfils

Winning in Business

Bruno Monfils

—

As a COO and angel investor, Bruno's passion lies in developing teams and building organizational foundations for business growth

"Employees who believe
that management
is concerned about them
as a whole person
– not just an employee –
are more productive, more
satisfied, more fulfilled.
Satisfied employees mean
satisfied customers,
which leads to profitability."

Anne M. Mulcahy,
CEO of Xerox

Winning in business is about seeing each individual in the organization as a gem of inestimable value. When we acknowledge our nobility, our oneness, and we see each other as parts of the whole, we can then redefine the meaning of success for a business and become agents of change for the betterment of all humanity.

Historically, businesses tend to head in the opposite direction, focused solely on advancing their financial goals and disregarding any other issues. All too often, the approach leaders use is the one that is the most comfortable for them – old, outworn methods that don't match the chosen strategy with the needs of the employees, the business units involved or, more broadly, the organization itself. The old way of doing business relies heavily on top-down strategies and decision-making processes that dictate and control.

Nowadays, however, more and more enlightened companies are realizing the simple fact that winning in business cannot happen when employees are disengaged and dissatisfied. Success comes when your primary focus moves away from dominance to a bottom-up management style that relies on trust and on the empowerment of your team members. The role of leaders is gradually changing: instead of dictating their company's strategy, today's leaders empower individuals to maximize the value they create for the organization.

It's all about connecting to the soul of your company and its purpose. You need to ask yourself two crucial questions: How is my company contributing to the betterment of its employees? Is it having a positive impact on society? If you apply this type of approach as a leader and as a team member, you will lift all the others, who will in turn lift you up, in a virtuous circle that will inevitably lead you and the entire team and company to a successful outcome.

The empowerment mindset needs to be instilled into your company culture, because building an empowerment-oriented business environment is a winning formula all around. According to a report by McKinsey & Company, the most successful companies are those whose managers and leaders become role models of the type of mindset and behavior that promotes empowerment. The report goes on to state that managers should display, communicate, and build the coaching skills they want to see in others. For smarter decisions, you need to empower your employees.

PEOPLE-FIRST LEADERSHIP

People-first leadership is directly linked to how engaged your team members are at work. Not getting it right is a sure way to demoralize your employees, which is bound to lead to poor team performance. Whenever employees are disengaged from their activities, a loss in productivity and revenue ensues. In the words of Sir Richard Branson, founder of The Virgin Group, "Clients do not come first. Employees come first. If you take care of your employees, they will take care of the clients."

In my different roles as operations leader and more recently at Amazon, I have learned that being a people-first leader and putting customers and employees first is a very contagious phenomenon. I have experienced people leadership on very different scales, from a dozen employees reporting to me all the way to ten thousand people. The fact that I've personally engaged with employees as well as with customers and the fact that I see them as the catalyst for real growth has generated well-being and success for all stakeholders involved. In one instance, this kind of approach made a team move from disillusionment to enthusiasm, as they found true meaning in being of service to each other and winning together. In other instances, some employees went as far as to say that they gained faith in senior leadership.

Putting people first boosts employee engagement, which in turn drives improvements in:

- Retention rates
- Job satisfaction and morale
- Output
- Quality
- Productivity
- Customer satisfaction
- Revenue and bottom-line profits.

Employees are far less likely to leave a workplace when they feel a sense of belonging and an emotional connection with their colleagues. Having a friendly and a community-like atmosphere at work creates a higher level of commitment to their jobs. As a result, job performance improves.

A people-first leader creates a sense of belonging and an inclusive company culture by placing a high value on the potential of all employees. According to a recent article by BetterUp, a leading executive coaching company, "Meaning, purpose, and belonging awaken potential. Our research shows that, above salary and job title, supporting the development of meaning for individuals leads to job satisfaction and commitment and protects against toxicity, stress, and burnout that eat away at performance and productivity. A feeling of belonging is even more important to engagement, long-term development, and contribution to teams."

Therefore, leaders and organizations need to change their approach, moving away from point solutions and toward human-centric, inclusive cultures that highlight the unique value of what each team member brings to the table.

THE "HOW CAN I HELP?" ATTITUDE

If you want to adopt a people-first approach, you need to take steps to demonstrate that people really are your top priority. A good way to start is by asking your team this simple question: "How can I help?".

Naturally, this is the easy part. The harder part is finding the time to actually listen to what your employees are saying. This will require some effort on your part, especially in the beginning, but it will get easier over time. It's all about caring enough to empathize with others, but the empathy muscle needs to be developed and strengthened. You will need to engage in active listening and show that you genuinely care. It's important to see your employees as human beings – imperfect, not always at their best, but striving to do what they can each day with what they have been given. You should try to understand and meet them where they are at in the present moment, because being present and in the moment is vital.

People First Productivity Solutions, an organization that has been at the forefront of helping companies with people development and boosting productivity since 2006, recommends that the leaders and managers of forward-thinking organizations that want to put people first implement the following action steps:

Get to know your employees and let them know you. It's important to interact with them human-to-human, not boss-to-subordinate.

Value their input and show interest in their different points of view. Instead of making unilateral decisions, listen attentively to what they have to say before reaching any conclusions.

- Encourage your employees' professional development by giving them plenty of learning opportunities and providing helpful feedback. Keep the communication channels open and actively seek ways to help their career.
- Make sure you provide all the information they need to understand the context and purpose of any tasks you assign. This will give your team a sense of belonging and strong motivation.
- All changes should be clearly explained, without neglecting to consider people's emotional responses. It takes time for any change to be accepted, so you need to be understanding in the beginning.
- Try to put yourself in other people's shoes when you speak to them or make decisions that will affect their work environment and well-being.

- Don't forget that it's in your own interest to treat your employees right, because your organization will reap the benefits if they're happy and engaged and suffer the consequences if they feel mistreated and disaffected.

We are in the process of building a new way of working that is inextricably linked to our well-being for generations to come – one where human transformation is possible for everyone, and everyone has a partner in their journey of growth. Each individual is seen as a protagonist and valued for the gems that they are: their very humanness, the essence of their being is supported and all their contributions nurtured. Building the future of our companies is an integral part of creating an ever-advancing civilization driven by soul-driven humans for the betterment of all.

Profits come when you put people first. This is the new way of leading organizations and businesses, regardless of whether you're just starting out as an entrepreneur/startup or you're a well-established corporation with thousands of employees.

CHALLENGING QUESTIONS

- Have you sensed a general lack of motivation in your company lately? If so, have you set aside some time to reflect on it?
- When was the last time you engaged in active listening with your team members, allowed them to share their insights and encouraged their input on how they would like to tackle a particular task or project?
- Have you ever sat down with one of your team members and just gotten to know them on a personal level, engaging in a meaningful conversation?
- If you are a business owner or a leader in an organization, how are you taking care of your staff?
- Can you think of a few innovative actions you would like to implement with your team in the future?

ABOUT THE AUTHOR

Bruno has over 20 years of leadership experience in Finance, Consulting and Operations thanks to senior roles in startups, scale-ups and multinationals. Having managed global teams and complex operations, he is passionate about coaching people, developing organizations to maturity and building process foundations for business growth. He spends his time investing in and advising leaders in high potential early-stage ventures and serving as Chief Operating Officer in a tech scale-up.

The Keys to Successfully Managing a Family Business: Gender Equity, Justice and Participation

Laura Grassi

—

Founder of Grassroots Facilitation

"Profit for a company is
like oxygen for a person.
If you don't have
enough of it, you're
out of the game.
But if you think
your life is about
breathing, you're really
missing something."

Peter Drucker

THE IMPACT OF RELATIONSHIPS ON FAMILY BUSINESSES

When family-owned businesses go through a period of transition or major changes, the people involved face some particularly difficult challenges and commonly experience the feeling of being stuck.

In this type of situation, it's important for family members to come together as a leadership team, in order to better understand the dynamics that are hindering progress in their organization. Oftentimes family-owned companies are mainly focused on business issues, but it's also essential to consider the impact of family relationships on the way they do business and on their ability to offer the world a valuable service and a great product.

Over the years I have noticed that family-owned businesses tend to follow a common pattern. After the founders have developed a wonderful and original idea into a business, that idea evolves and is passed on from generation to generation, often growing into what appears to be a very successful business. However, at a certain point the company goes through a moment of crisis, in which the original principles of the business and the initial ideas on how to make a meaningful contribution don't match the current reality, or the way the business is structured internally is no longer suitable for getting the work done in an effective way.

Most of the time, the solution cannot be found by just looking at the business aspects – i.e., restructuring the organization, changing the strategy or the products that are being offered. The key to a successful outcome is going back to the origins of the company and looking at how family relationships have influenced the business and created dynamics that are still having an impact on the organization. These dynamics often get in the way of a better flow, hindering prosperity and a more just way of organizing the business internally.

HOW TO HAVE A DIFFERENT CONVERSATION ABOUT YOUR BUSINESS

I have extensive personal experience of these issues through the family company that my great-grandfather founded. When I took part in business conversations with my family, I realized how important it was to involve the different shareholders – who happened to be my uncles, my sisters and my dad – in a deep and meaningful discussion of the essential values of the company we had inherited. It's essential to be really bold as well as honest in these types of conversations, asking questions like "What values do we want to bring forward?" and "How can we treat each other fairly?", rather than just looking at spreadsheets. We had been focusing on the business side of things for a long time, but this was not enough to achieve the results we wanted. Therefore, it became clear to me that we also needed to consider family-related issues.

That's how I learned what types of conversation need to happen at each stage, and how important it is to find the courage to bring challenging issues to the table. Now my mission is to help other family-owned businesses overcome their difficulties and thrive.

I contribute to their success by supporting and coaching mindful leaders to have a different conversation about their businesses, not just on the usual level, which is mostly about strategy, but on a value level. My role is to offer guidance and support throughout these difficult conversations about family issues. Here are some of the powerful questions that need to be asked:

- What does this company mean for us?
- What were its original values?
- Have the original intentions been preserved?
- What are the gifts that have been created?
- What are the challenges that have emerged?

Perhaps management teams haven't been able to address these issues because of their double role, which involves both a business relationship and a family relationship.

By using different approaches, like family constellations, system constellations, and facilitation of participatory dialogue, we can really bring a different conversation to the table, including unspoken elements and especially things that are difficult to talk about. It's important to create a safe space that allows these aspects to become part of the conversation that takes place on the business level.

The ultimate goal is to create better conditions for family-owned businesses to be prosperous, just, healthy, and meaningful, reconnecting to the full potential of a business idea that shouldn't only provide a benefit to the shareholders but also bring prosperity and justice to all the stakeholders involved.

This involves rethinking the relationship between employers and employees, reconsidering how resources are used, and finding more meaningful and ethical ways to reshape the business.

WHAT VALUES CAN THESE SAFE SPACES UNLEASH?

Developing these safe spaces can unlock creativity as well as a new understanding of what the business could look like in the future. The strong family values that emerge in the course of these conversations can then be brought into the business in ways that benefit everybody.

The value of justice creates a safe space where the management team has a chance to discuss what's just and fair for the business, and how the business treats all the individuals involved.

The value of gender equity is also important, because businesses have traditionally been run following a top-down masculine approach, while now we understand the impact of relationships and we are able to build a sense of community that leads to a healthier work environment.

Finally, the value of participation means that businesses are not just focused on a strategic mindset, but are also able to adopt a relational viewpoint.

The two tips I would like to share are the following:

- Business is never just about business: it's also about relationships and how to reconnect these two aspects.
- Trust the process: it's a path that brings more unity, equity and justice. It means that we can be guided through these steps by a higher power – the original intention of creating something meaningful for the world, which was the idea that was embraced in the first place when the business was founded. That original intention can still be kept alive, as long as we have an open and honest conversation on how this reflects on the current situation.

I believe that individuals naturally feel a need to find meaning and contribute to the common good. Through my work I provide tools and programs to support individuals in this journey of self-discovery and empowerment. I support organizations and companies in creating an environment where fulfillment, purpose and contribution can thrive and prosper. I am passionate about creating spaces for human interaction. I believe that it is through interaction with other people that we are able to fully develop our talents and skills and find a meaningful way to use them.

CHALLENGING QUESTIONS

- What does this company mean for you and your family?
- What were the original values of the company?
- How have the original intentions been transmitted from generation to generation?
- What are the values you want to bring forward?
- What is the fairest way to treat each other within the family and the organization?
- What results do you want to achieve, in alignment with the vision of your business and the goal of serving a higher purpose?

ABOUT THE AUTHOR

Laura supports organizations and communities to navigate the complexity of the work they do by fostering collaboration and creating an environment characterized by participation, engagement and trust. Over the past 10 years she has worked with local governments, European institutions, developmental NGOs, philanthropic organizations and social enterprises, to support them in working collaboratively and address our most pressing societal issues through a new lens of collaboration and active participation. In her work, Laura brings together different methodologies such as "The Art of Hosting Participatory Leadership", *U-theory, Process Design, Deep Democracy and NonViolent Communication in order to offer a unique approach to collaboration and organizational development.*

Building Bridges for Humanity with Impact Investment

Jenna Nicholas

—

Jenna Nicholas is a CEO, Stanford Business School alum and board member. Jenna uses impact investing as a tool to address the world's great challenges through investing and advisory work

"We stand on the threshold of an age whose convulsions proclaim alike the death-pangs of the old order and the birth-pangs of the new."

Shoghi Effendi

UBUNTU: "I AM BECAUSE WE ARE"

In a world teetering on the brink of profound change, the question of why we must engage in ethical business is answered by the tumultuous challenges we observe in our societies. With a significant $82 trillion invested globally, it's staggering that less than 2% reaches companies and firms led and owned by women and people of color. This disparity shows the critical need for heightened awareness and a strategic approach to investment that challenges and changes the status quo.

Ethical business models can be the incubators for a world where economic decisions honor human dignity and ensure social equity. The how we do it, is a meticulous endeavor to blend our core values into everything our organizations do, making sure our actions and choices truly reflect our commitment to justice and equity. By consciously directing our efforts towards inclusivity we not only foster fairness but also empower the underrepresented voices in business and finance, which is vital for the enrichment of our collective future.

This process challenges us to overcome biases and assumptions that often distort our judgment and decisions. It necessitates a deep, inward reflection on how our organizations live out these principles, as well as an outward look at our interactions with wider communities. That is exactly what my work involves: creating partnerships with other organizations and establishing meaningful connections with communities that have historically been marginalized.

In my own journey, I've come to realize the potent intersection of spirituality with business as a fundamental element for creating an ethical and purposeful environment. Such environments are *intentional spaces* where people can bring their whole selves, with their different reasons for why they do what they do, spaces where every individual's contribution is valued and diversity is seen as richness. Building bridges across the divides of race, gender, social standing, economic background, and religion can craft work environments that genuinely honor diversity and foster opportunities for connection. The process of *"bridge-building"* within organizations and communities – creating relationships grounded in deep respect for individuals' varied backgrounds and life experiences – fosters environments that honor the full spectrum of human experience and aspiration.

Bridge-building is a concept deeply rooted in the South African philosophy of *Ubuntu*, which translates to *"I am because we are"*. This idea encourages us to see ourselves as part of a larger interconnected web, understanding that the well-being and success of one entity are interdependent with others. It's a perspective that shifts our definition of success from individual victories to collective triumphs, promoting a win-win approach over a zero-sum game.

From this viewpoint, success isn't a solitary achievement but a shared experience. To actualize this, it's crucial to invest time in truly understanding what success means for everyone involved, which means setting aside our preconceived notions and engaging with an open mind and heart.

BRIDGING WORLDS THROUGH HUMAN CONNECTIONS

Raised in London and inspired by my studies in international relations, as well as earning an MBA at Stanford, I was drawn early to the intersection of business and social impact – a blend of financial savvy with a commitment to social and environmental progress. My thesis on impact investing in China marked the beginning of my journey alongside pioneers of socially responsible investment, where I observed a disconnect between investors and the communities they aimed to help.

It was this gap that inspired me to co-found *Impact Experience.* We aim to bridge the gap between investors, entrepreneurs, and often overlooked communities, working on equity across various sectors such as investments, climate, healthcare, and education. Previously, I created a coalition of 170 foundations managing $50 billion in assets under management, redirecting capital from fossil fuels to innovative, sustainable solutions.

The importance of bridge-building in business was deepened by my work leading Impact Experience. Whether it is Montgomery, Alabama, Southern West Virginia, or New Orleans, I've seen the profound impact of truly understanding the communities and individuals we engage with.

During the Impact Experiences we organize, we gather diverse groups – investors, entrepreneurs, community partners – and begin by sharing something meaningful, a symbol or an object. This practice allows us to connect on a human level first, before professional roles define our interactions. It opens doors to collaborations built on a foundation of mutual understanding and respect, celebrating the fullness of each individual's humanity.

I remember a particular occasion where I found myself facilitating a dialogue between a former coal miner and a renewable energy business person. The coal miner brought a piece of coal to our meeting, not just as a symbol of his livelihood, but his identity. The renewable energy business person, in contrast, presented a solar panel. On the surface, they could not have been more different. Yet, as they spoke, it became evident that their core motivations – family, community, a better future – were strikingly similar. This was a defining moment for me because it demonstrated the power of understanding and respecting diverse narratives, forming a bridge beyond industry differences and personal beliefs.

This approach was the driving force behind the creation of Impact Experience. We saw a need for deeper community integration within the business and investment sectors – spaces where authentic connections could flourish. When we engage deeply with communities, we're better positioned to address larger societal issues that affect both our work and our lives.

ACHIEVING UNITY: THE CORE PRINCIPLES

Bridge-building is very much achievable. It's about being present, intentional, and willing to engage with others as complete individuals, beyond just their roles. It means more than simply avoiding conflict; it enriches connections and, ultimately, our collective progress. The principles that underpin the ethos of business and bridge-building are anchored in the rich soil of inclusivity, respect, and genuine collaboration.

- As mentioned, the foundation lies in the principle of **Ubuntu**, a beautiful South African notion that translates to *"I am because we are"*. It's a recognition of our interconnectedness and interdependence. This principle of unity is vital for both individuals and organizations because it shifts the paradigm from a zero-sum game to a collective success model. So the advice is simple yet profound: Begin by genuinely understanding others as human beings. Recognize their needs, aspirations, and motivations without the interference of biases.
- **Consultation and collaboration** are other bedrocks of this approach. In a world that's increasingly polarized, creating spaces where people can come together despite differing viewpoints is crucial. This means celebrating the diversity of thought, experience, and background, and understanding that this diversity enriches rather than divides.
- Moreover, the principle of **intentionality in building relationships** is foundational. It's about reaching beyond our familiar circles and making the effort to understand the

perspectives and needs of others, especially those who have been historically marginalized or overlooked.

- In the rush of our daily routines, we often forget to lay the groundwork for our interactions, leading to misunderstandings. Through Impact Experience, we emphasize the importance of **spending time with community members and partners** – knowing their families, their stories, and their lives beyond the surface. This investment in relationship-building is not only enriching but essential; it fosters better relationships and ensures more effective and meaningful partnerships. By allocating time upfront, we're acting proactively, creating a solid base for future collaboration and reducing potential conflicts.
- **Reflective practice** is also key. It involves examining the impact of our actions, being aware of the traces we leave behind, and ensuring they align with the values we espouse. This kind of introspection ensures that our business practices are not only effective but also ethical and sustainable.
- Finally, there's the principle of **action-oriented engagement.** It's not enough to have dialogues; the true measure of our commitment to these values is how they translate into tangible actions and outcomes that benefit not just the organization but society at large. We must embody the change we wish to see, creating ripples of impact through every decision and interaction.

These principles, when applied, serve as a compass, guiding businesses towards practices that not only yield economic prosperity but also contribute to the betterment of society. They demand that we not only envision a future that honors our shared humanity but actively participate in its creation.

FORGING REAL CONNECTIONS TO TRANSFORM THE WORLD

Applying the principles of ethical business and bridge-building within an organization catalyzes profound transformation. It is a shift from insularity to inclusivity, from transactional to transformational interactions.

At Impact Experience, we gather investors and businesses every few months to deeply delve into the historical context, examining the persistent effects of structural racism that manifest in present-day issues, such as mass incarceration, police brutality and bias in the asset management industry. We immerse ourselves in the community, engaging deeply with individuals affected by long-standing inequities, tracing the lineage from past atrocities to current challenges in wealth distribution. During our engagements, we weave together intensive multi-day sessions that involve symbol sharing and the arts to forge a real connection between participants. This culminates in tangible commitments for future actions, with a follow-through that underpins the entire experience. Our work goes beyond having conversations; it aims at reallocating capital towards businesses run by women and people of color, promoting a shift in how capital is invested and influencing behavioral changes towards broader business practices. These concerted efforts lead to a tangible impact in communities like Montgomery, New Orleans, and others, where we work towards a future where resources and opportunities are distributed more equitably and thoughtfully.

In the larger context, the ripple effect of such transformation can be significant for many other people and businesses. Companies become role models, challenging industry norms and inspiring others to follow suit. This can lead to broader societal changes, influencing policy, and shaping the future of business. Transformation through ethical business is not just about doing good; it's about being better – better leaders, better colleagues, better stewards of the planet to create a legacy that speaks to the kind of future we aspire to leave for the next generations.

FOSTERING INTEGRATION IN SOCIETY FOR A NEW WORLD ORDER

The concept of bridge-building resonates with me on a profound level due to its capacity to unify seemingly disparate entities – business, community, and personal values. The importance of this topic emerges from my deep-seated belief in the oneness of humanity, a principle central to the Bahá'í Faith, which informs much of my work and worldview. This principle is not just theoretical; it's a call to action that demands we acknowledge our interconnectedness and the impact of our economic decisions on society. Through my work, I've seen how business can either exacerbate divisions or become a conduit for healing and unity. Whether it's addressing racial equity, investing in sustainable practices, or elevating marginalized voices, the way we conduct business can be a powerful force for positive change.

The Bahá'í Faith acknowledges the forces of disintegration and integration that exist within the world. In today's world, the media often highlights the crumbling, disintegrative aspects of society. Yet, equally present are the forces of integration, which ethical businesses can amplify. By fostering these integrative forces, we contribute to the foundation of a new world order. This transformation requires bridge-building efforts like directing capital towards communities of color, crucial for heralding this new era of change.

When considering the business world's role in this integration process, it's clear that the moral dimension isn't distant from business at all. In fact, ethical business is integral to constructing this new world. Every industry, from education to healthcare, is touched by business, and thus, ethical considerations within business practices become essential. By holding ourselves accountable to ethical standards, we pave the way for a transition into a more ethical, unified way of existence.

WHAT YOU CAN DO

- **Embrace Ubuntu:** Start every partnership by recognizing the humanity in each other. Understand what success means to your collaborators and build from that common ground.
- **Invest Time in Relationships:** Take the time to understand and appreciate the diverse backgrounds and perspectives of those you engage with, setting the stage for a more profound collaboration. Investing time in building relationships with individuals from diverse backgrounds requires intentionality and a willingness to step outside our comfort zones.
- **Consult:** approach these interactions with a mindset of seeking to understand and learn, rather than imposing our own perspectives, facilitates meaningful dialogue.
- Often, we gravitate towards those who share similar backgrounds or perspectives without realizing; instead, we have an opportunity to consciously reach beyond our immediate circles to engage with people from different backgrounds. **Diversity in decision-making processes**, whether in boardrooms or partnerships, is proven to lead to superior outcomes. Research underscores the advantages of diverse perspectives, highlighting the untapped potential of inclusivity in driving innovation and success. Hence, embracing diversity is not only a moral obligation, but also a strategic advantage, ensuring comprehensive perspectives and maximizing potential for positive outcomes.

CHALLENGING QUESTIONS

- In what ways can you or your organization become more actively involved in addressing issues of racial equity, sustainable practices, and elevating marginalized voices within your industry?
- Identify a community or group that has been historically marginalized within your sphere of influence. What tangible actions can you take to engage with and support this community?
- When was the last time you stepped outside your comfort zone to build a relationship with someone from a different background? How do you currently invest in understanding the backgrounds and values of your colleagues and partners?

ABOUT THE AUTHOR

Jenna Nicholas is the co-founder and CEO of Impact Experience which is focused on addressing structural racism by confronting and engaging with the historical and ongoing realities of inequality and racial bias. She also spearheads the Business for Climate Finance initiative through Impact Experience to decarbonize corporate bank accounts and retirement funds.

Jenna leads Investments and Acquisitions for One Planet Group which incubates, operates, and invests in businesses. Jenna formerly founded Phoenix Global Impact, a firm that specializes in impact investing, social entrepreneurship, and strategic philanthropy. Through her firm, she project-managed Divest-Invest Philanthropy, a coalition of foundations, divesting from investments in fossil fuels and reinvesting in new economy solutions. Jenna spoke at TedXPortland about the Divest-Invest work. Jenna has also worked with the World Bank Treasury on green bonds and other sustainability projects and with Toniic helping to support an impact investing community. She has worked closely with the Calvert Special Equities team, actively investing in companies and funds in the areas of education technology, financial inclusion, renewable energy, and sustainable agriculture.

Jenna graduated from Stanford University with an International Relations Honors Degree during which time she also read International Development at Oxford University. Jenna is a Stanford Graduate School of Business MBA graduate, a PD Soros Fellow for New Americans, recipient of the Stanford Social Innovation Fellowship, an Echoing Green Fellow, Forbes 30 under 30 for Social Entrepreneurship. Jenna has also served on the Impact Advisory Committee for Apollo Global Management. She is an active member of the Baháí Faith.

Reconsidering Leadership with Systemic Thinking

Andreas Galsterer

—

The idea of a world in unity fascinates and motivates him at the same time. Andreas applies his knowledge to Systemic Organisational & Leadership Development

"Systemic thinking, social
learning, teamwork
and personal integrity are
the distinguishing features
of a new phase
of development
in humankind, bearing
all the signs of integrative
levels of maturity."

Kambiz Poostchi

Once upon a time, there was a wise old man who lived in a small village. He was known for his wisdom and his wise advice. One day, a young man came to him and asked him how to best make his dreams come true. The wise man told him, "My son, you must understand that dreams do not come true by mere wishing. To reach your dreams, you must be willing to take the necessary steps and put in the effort to make them happen." The wise man went on to explain that the journey to success was not easy, but it was worth it. He explained, "Success is a process, not an event. You must be willing to work towards you mission, overcome obstacles, and persist even when you are faced with failure. There is no easy road to it, but with the right attitude and determination, anything is possible."

The young man thanked him for his advice, and then went off to put it into practice. With his newfound understanding of the importance of the process, he was able to take the necessary steps and eventually achieved his dreams. And so, the wise man's words of wisdom still ring true to this day: "Success is a process, not an event".

WHAT IS SYSTEMIC THINKING?

Nowadays, one of the main challenges that corporations are facing is a general feeling of dissatisfaction and a lack of intrinsic motivation among workers. In the constant pressure of meeting deadlines and achieving results the process is oftentimes neglected.

Conflicts in the workplace are becoming more frequent and what is commonly known as the Great Resignation is now affecting most companies.

It's important to see these phenomena as symptoms rather than causes of the current situation, because it is only by understanding their root causes that we can change the course of future events.

This requires an urgent solution. Albert Einstein remarked: *"We cannot solve our problems with the same level of thinking that created them."* Therefore, these challenges will only be solved by adopting a new level of thinking.

We are entering the century of maturity, in which every person can make their own independent decisions and take responsibility for them. Hierarchical structures, where power is usually concentrated in a small group of people in the top of the organization, used to be the norm in the corporate world. But in today's complex and interdependent world, these traditional, highly inflexible approaches are becoming increasingly obsolete.

The focus is to create environments which enable a shift from power to empowerment, from control to contribution, from centralized to decentralized systems. These shifts require us to look at our organizations as an open system instead of a static structure. This is a profound change, where we identify and acknowledge the contribution that each subject can make. It's an innovative way of achieving growth and development, based on reciprocity and interconnectedness. While defying categorization as either "top-down" or "bottom-up", this approach leads to a nurturing and supportive environment that empowers team members to achieve their highest potential, explore new possibilities and co-create a different reality.

In his book *"The Sense of the Whole. From the Fragmented Present to a Systemic Future"* Kambiz Poostchi, the author and creator of *"The Open System Model"* (OSM) outlines what an open system is and how to work with it through understanding the underlying social dynamics. He provides remarkable insights into patterns of social change and failing societies, as well as into challenges such as business mergers or patchwork families.

The core of the systemic model recognizes how important it is for an organization of any kind to establish a coherent mission, pursue a common purpose, and build a shared vision with the belief that we are stronger if we work together. It also stresses how management can change from the carrot principle of extrinsic reward models and instead support their employees through meaning and intrinsic motivation.

The existence and potential of a system only emerges from a strong alignment towards the respective, comprehensive whole. It means focusing on the big picture and the general principles rather than single components or events. With the systemic approach, it is possible to explain previously only sensed yet misunderstood undesirable developments and to align previously unconnected matters. By doing so, the focus is mainly on relationships and connections. Even if these are not always visible, measurable, or quantifiable they still represent the real core of system understanding.

Since the world has radically changed, we must radically change our thinking – this is what the systemic approach is all about. A new way of understanding the complexity of a system, including corporations, a department, a team or a family. It is looking at the course of its multi-layered, systemic order.

THE THREE ORDERS OF SYSTEMIC THINKING

The Open System Model differentiates between three different orders of Systemic Thinking. Precisely because the term "systemic" is currently often used as an empty phrase, it is necessary for the practical development of system competencies to be aware of the phases or levels of order of systemic consciousness that build on one another.

Systemic Thinking First Order — Thinking in Networks

The first order is called "Thinking in Networks". This means that when we work together, individuals construct their identities through their network of relationships. The human consciousness leaves the confines of egocentricity, and experiences that higher quality results can be achieved by working together. Results achieved at this level are not subject to the wear and tear of struggle and strife but are summative in nature. This means that they arise from harmonious additions from the talents and potentials from each individual within the network. At this stage it is all about cooperation.

Despite increasing enthusiasm for "thinking in networks", which can be seen by the huge amount of on and offline events such as after-work get togethers etc., over time the limits and weaknesses at this order of thinking become apparent. As a logical consequence from the awareness which arises from the sense of "all-connectedness", competitive thinking and comparison don't make sense anymore. However, this approach lacks the necessary immunity against such destructive influences. At this level of thinking the individual is still focused on "self" and lacks the capacity to work on his relationships, leading to fragmentation and conflicting group interests.

Systemic Thinking Second Order — Holistic Thinking

The second order is known as the "Holistic Approach". This is a significant expansion of network thinking. This emphasizes the fact that we are all part of something bigger, be it a community, a family, or a company. The individual understands that their contribution is necessary and important. When we learn to see and appreciate the bigger picture, we can make the transition and become its supporter. Employees which achieve this level of consciousness receive responsibilities within the system.

Here we start to talk about "team" development. Team development from a systemic point of view, has less to do with organizational structures but is more a result of the systemic maturity of its members. As the same word "team" is often used for working groups, the potential of real teams cannot be distinguished.

If the individual, however, has a broader intention, for example in the role of a parent in a family system, as an executive in a company or as a teacher in a classroom, to take responsibility for the system and thus for the course of the system (and not only within the system), the limitations and restrictions of holistic thinking become apparent.

Systemic Thinking Third Order — Thinking in Levels

The third order is "Thinking in Levels" or "Open System Thinking". "Thinking in Levels" builds upon the network and holistic approach. It follows the principle of the multi-layered nature of open systems. A team can be a sub-system of a department, a department is a sub-system of a company, a company is a sub-system of society as a whole. An open or aligned system is thus viewed as a complex whole, which derives its particular character trait, specific features, and emergent attributes from its unique alignment to the overarching system. From this functional role with meaning and purpose within the larger system, springs its distinctive identity and form.

The thrust and motivation for such a process is the potential of intrinsically motivated and entrepreneurially minded employees, so-called “intrapreneurs” – entrepreneurs within companies. Such employees are not only effective for themselves or in their cooperative network, but are also able to take responsibility for the shared vision. It is evident that the promotion of interdependence between the members of the system is one of the essential prerequisites as we want to leave old hierarchical structures, be they organizational or social, behind. This opens spaces for participative, more mature and decentralized structures.

All the information and the ideas which spring from the higher system transform themselves into energy and enthusiasm, eventually leading to the creation of a project, a service or a product. Consequently, the final output is inextricably linked to the higher system. In the context of a company, every department should always focus on how it’s contributing to the company as a whole, in unity and with meaning. For everything there is a degree of maturity and perfection. The maturity level of systemic thinking is the expression of the consciousness of interdependence.

To identify our true contribution, i.e., our mission, it is essential to understand the three orders of Systemic Thinking.

LEARNING ORGANIZATIONS & THE THREE SYSTEMIC PRINCIPLES

Systemic Thinking is based on three core principles: The principle of order, the principle of affiliation and the principle of awareness. These three principles, just like natural laws, interrelate with each other. They should be seen as the basis of a coherent perspective, reflecting the basic human needs of love, will and the quest for knowledge. They can be regarded as prerequisites for human growth, creativity, and fulfilment. They lead to the realization and appreciation of human unity. Ignoring these three principles may lead to resignation, sullenness or fluctuation.

If the whole is going well, the parts need to benefit, too. By doing so it maintains its order (the principle of order). Out of the necessity of the search of meaning and sense-making, the principle of awareness rises. In an affiliation scenario, where everyone is part of a company, you need to create a sense of belonging, valuing the differences and appreciating new perspectives in alignment with the needs of the higher system (the principle of affiliation).

"How to make a meaningful contribution to society and how to get every member of the organization to work toward the same goal" is the challenge that all companies are facing today. Bill O'Brien, former president of Hannover Insurance Company, was one of the first proponents of the concept of the learning organization. He believes that traditional hierarchical organizations are unable to satisfy their employees' higher order needs, such as self-respect and self-actualization, and advocates more flexible organizational models.

Today's companies still tend to apply a "reward and punishment method", based on how accurately their workers follow instructions rather than how they volunteer their unique gifts to make their contribution. This method doesn't involve any type of exchange: I tell you what to do – and possibly even how you should do it, because that's the way I would do it. If you don't do it or you do it in a different way, you're either wrong or not performing well.

This generates frustration, because if things don't work out, it means that you didn't do them properly, i.e., you didn't follow the instructions in the correct way. On the other hand, if all goes well, you cannot take any credit because I told you what to do. I am the hero, while you are just the executor. I will reap all the benefits; you just did your job. This is clearly unhealthy and demotivating. In the long run, conflicts arise, dissatisfied employees and demotivated workers will either check-out (quit quitting) or leave the company, trying to find a more rewarding environment where they are valued.

If we teach people to be controlled instead of leading themselves, we are missing a great opportunity and our society is bound to suffer. We'll end up perpetuating the rigid mindset of the industrial age, to follow instructions, that we often learn in traditional family structures or within the school system etc. While companies tend to recognize the value of cooperation, equality, inclusion, sharing and team building, the sad truth is that most organizations are still living by the old paradigm of competition and solely making profits. However at the next promotional charity event opportunity, the check is handed over stating how generously "we are planting trees for the planet".

SYSTEMIC LEADERSHIP

Systemic Leadership requires a total change in perspective. It is not based on position, status, or superiority. Instead from a systemic point of view, leadership is a function which has to bear responsibility for the whole. This means for Systemic Leadership a comprehensive awareness and systemic thinking competence of a higher order is necessary.

While, for example, for management tasks an inner knowledge of the structural order may be sufficient, Systemic Leadership is a responsibility which arises from the awareness of the principles of systemic thinking. Therefore, those can be regarded as pre-requisites for successful leadership where the human being in his diversity and the unique contribution of each individual is appreciated and necessary for the success of the whole. If the function of leadership is missing or weakened, this development leads to the destabilization of the whole system, which consequently can manifest itself through manifold symptoms on different structural levels.

Therefore leadership must lead. By doing so leaders are accountable not only for their own organization, but essentially for all the repercussions that the work of the organization has on the higher systems. Systemic Leadership means realizing that there is no planet B. We need to consider the whole and not just our single objective. Systemic Leadership helps managers and companies understand how they can and should use their leadership, ideas, and skills to support the whole organization and ultimately benefit the wider community. It also helps organizations become more aware of their role within society.

It's essentially a paradigm shift that leads away from an outworn industrial age leadership mindset toward an innovative, more holistic approach. The main benefits of this transformation are:

1. It leads to more unity and alignment within a company, as well as a functional understanding of what people are doing and why they are doing it.
2. It makes company leaders and managers aware of systemic core principles. Thus, it is a practical framework to distinguish the root cause of the symptoms. This enables them to distinguish between what is urgent and essential for the good of the company and what can wait.
3. It highlights the difference between leadership and management, which clarifies how to set up systems that support this approach in every level of the company.

By adopting this approach, you take responsibility for who you are and what you are, defining your role and nurturing your higher capacity. By giving you the tools to be empowered in your everyday decision-making process, Systemic Thinking will impact your personal and professional life for the better, not to mention the lives of all the people around you.

NEXT STEPS TO EMBARK TO LEAD SYSTEMICALLY

It's important to identify your contribution and apply this approach in a way that works for you, so that you can implement the changes successfully. There are a few questions you should reflect upon when you decide to adopt a systemic leadership style:

- What are the current needs of the overarching higher system? Society, company, department? Can you pinpoint them and list them? Find as many as you can and prioritize them.
- For which of those needs, do you want to take responsibility? This is your mission, your mandate.
- Would it make a difference if you weren't contributing to this specific need in the higher system (your region, community etc.)? What is the contribution you are making? Is it meaningful and does it make sense? This is your purpose.
- How does your contribution change the higher system in which you operate? Visualize this in rich detail. This is your vision.
- Who are you as a company when you are embarking in alignment with your mission? This is your corporate identity.

"It is a matter of making a joint effort to learn how to integrate the diversity of nations, cultures, religions, and economic systems, in the course of an organic transformation process, into a functional wholeness."

Kambiz Poostchi.

CHALLENGING QUESTIONS

- How can you apply the principle of "Thinking in Networks" within your current team or community to foster a more cooperative and harmonious environment?
- Identify an area in your life or work where adopting a "Holistic Approach" could improve your understanding of your role within the larger system. What specific action will you take to support this transition?
- Reflecting on the "Thinking in Levels" concept, how can you better align your daily actions with the overarching goals of your organization or community to contribute to a cohesive and meaningful shared vision?
- Considering the principles of systemic thinking, what steps can you take to exhibit systemic leadership, regardless of your role, to contribute to the well-being of the larger system you are part of?

ABOUT THE AUTHOR

As an independent consultant, trainer and coach since 2020, Andreas specialised in Systemic Leadership & Team Development to support organisational change and transformational processes. He is delighted when it comes to Systems Thinking & Strategy. In his words "It is thrilling to venture into unfamiliar territory, to go beyond the common place, the familiar, the obvious." *He is being recognised making unintelligible or complex ideas, plans, procedures or regulations easy to understand. Andreas entertains ideas about the best ways to reach a goal, increase productivity or solve a problem. He worked in South-Africa for the travel industry and later organised trainings & conferences world-wide from Australasia, Europe, over India to the Americas within the Med-Tech Industry.*

Andreas studied in Germany, Austria, Portugal and Brazil. He finalised with a Bachelor of Science in Sports Management. His finalised his Master Thesis in Strategic Management in New Zealand about the Rugby World Cup 2011 with the Initiative of the World Food Program (WFP).

Unleash Your Feminine Powers to Graceful Aging

Nooshin K. Darvish

—

Doctor in Naturopathic Medicine
Founder and chief medical officer of
the award-winning Holistique Medical Center

*"The male and female
are like the two wings
of a bird and when both
wings are reinforced
with the same impulse
the bird of humanity
will be enabled to soar
heavenward to the summit
of progress."*

'Abdu'l-Bahá,
*The Promulgation
of Universal Peace*

Businesses, at their core, are human endeavors with a soul. As such, the health and wellbeing of the individuals within these enterprises are not just personal concerns but are intrinsically linked to the overall sustainability and health of the business itself and, ultimately, to its broader impact on society. Workplace innovation, resilience, and excellence depend on the physical and mental health of people – the women and men whose talents, creativity, and labor are the lifeblood of any enterprise.

My journey as a licensed naturopathic physician and a business owner has taught me that the holistic wellbeing of the individual, intertwined with that of the business, is foundational to unleashing people's and the enterprise's full potential. In my quest for excellence, both personally and professionally, I have discovered that an alignment of mind, body, and soul within oneself and within the business is not just beneficial; it is essential. Such alignment serves as the cornerstone for building both a successful career and a fulfilling life. It is only when our physical health, mental clarity, and spiritual peace are in harmony and aligned with the values of the business, and vice versa, that we can manifest the best of ourselves as well as that of the organization. Such a holistic approach empowers us to progress through life and the complex world of business with resilience, empathy, and a clear sense of purpose.

Born in Tehran in 1969, I witnessed my mother's struggle to navigate the expectations of a patriarchal society while fostering a spirit of resilience and independence that she passed on to her future generations. This foundation of strength, audacity, patience and wisdom became a guiding light for me as I journeyed through my own path through immigration to Canada, medical training in the United States, and eventual recognition as a pioneering naturopathic doctor with an award-winning integrative medical practice. For the past 32 years since I married, at least ten close family members battled cancer, culminating in my mother's and father's unexpected passing during the COVID-19 pandemic. Journeying through such trials and tribulations with loved ones tested my faith and resilience, further deepening my understanding of life's fragility and the importance of living with purpose and integrity. My parents' legacy, coupled with the transformative experiences of perimenopause and the global upheaval of the pandemic impacting my personal and business life, spurred a period of intense self-reflection and renewal. I emerged with a renewed commitment and a deeper understanding of the importance of one's own wellbeing and its vital connection to the wellbeing of one's community and workplace.

The soulful interplay between health, spiritual fulfillment, and masculine and feminine energies within oneself and within organizations, imparts a fundamental element in creating gratifying careers and a personal life journey that benefits not only oneself but that of the business, its people and the society. This comprehensive approach to business involves prioritizing embracing spiritual values, such as service, intuition, forbearance, unity, empathy and compassion – all of which are feminine qualities often lacking in modern business practices – over profitability, greed and power – often acknowledged as masculine qualities. Consciously embodying the transformative feminine energies innately within every man and woman alongside the masculine energies, in one's personal life as well as in the values and culture of one's corporation, leads to personal joy, business sustainibility, resilience and success.

Today, as a woman business owner, pioneering an integrative medical practice while challenged by a male dominant business milieu, I have experienced that businesses based on harmony of feminine and masculine values and ideals are significantly more sustainable while positively impacting and transforming thousands of lives and the community. I've come to understand that womens' unique challenges and strengths position us to pioneer a future where ethical business practices can become the norm.

BECOME A GOLDEN GATE: EMBRACING FEMININE LEADERSHIP

Despite progress, women continue to confront numerous challenges in our age – gender discrimination and biases, balancing the demands of motherhood and work aspirations, and the physical and emotional toll of different life stages, from menstruation to menopause. In the relentless whirl of life – where roles as mothers, partners, professionals, and caregivers converge – women tirelessly balance the demands of personal and professional life. Expectations are incredibly high. However the journey of womanhood is adorned with trials and triumphs, each one a doorway to deeper understanding and inner growth. Every phase in life offers hidden blessings and growth opportunities that can shape women into exemplars of resilience.

There is a "Golden Gate" within each woman, a Supreme Consciousness, a reservoir of untapped power, urging us to rise above societal limitations and to embrace our authentic selves. The Golden Gate is what every woman has capacity to become: an enlightened, authentic agent of positive transformation who can unleash her feminine powers to create a better world for our future generations. It's a call to reject the diminutive voices that echo the antiquated beliefs of yesteryears and to recognize our indispensable role in society's advancement. We hold the key to be agents of change, architects of a world that honors the balance between masculine and feminine energies, as essential as the two wings of a bird, each vital for the flight toward collective progress.

Unleashing our feminine powers means tuning into the empathetic, nurturing, and intuitive traits inherent within us. It's about grounding ourselves in the present, shedding the ego that distorts reality, and stepping into a realm where right or wrong lose their dichotomy. We need to trust the natural unfolding of our abilities, which can lead and transform our lives, the business world, and the entire human civilization.

As women, aligning our inner compass towards balance positions us to lead society toward moderation, collaboration and harmony. Embracing our noble essence, we transcend the binaries of giver and taker, evolving into beings of creation and love, akin to noble gases that neither gain nor lose but exist in a state of completeness. Women possess both the opportunity and the responsibility to cultivate their inner beauty, wisdom, and power, embarking on their own journeys of self-discovery and healing. This path not only enables personal transformation but also aligns with a broader mission: to foster a world where women are celebrated for their contributions, resilience, and capacity to lead with compassion, creativity, and grace. By healing – mind, body, and soul – every woman can become a "Golden Gate": a feminine goddess equipped to guide the world out of its spiritual and material crisis towards a more just and peaceful society.

HEALTHY PEOPLE, HEALTHY BUSINESS: KEY PRINCIPLES FOR UNLOCKING HOLISTIC WELLBEING

The synergy between mind, body, and soul

Embracing feminine energy within the business sphere lays the groundwork for a leadership paradigm rooted in holistic wellbeing. A holistic approach to wellbeing is one that recognizes the intricate interplay between mind, body, and soul. This comprehensive approach underscores the synergy of this trinity, essential for cultivating resilient, insightful, and purpose-driven leaders who can navigate the challenges of modern business with empathy and integrity.

A healthy balance between this triad provides the energy and strength needed to pursue our ambitions. A *healthy body* fosters a healthy mind, enabling us to think clearly, make informed decisions, and lead with conviction. Nutrition, exercise, and rest prepare us to face the demands of the deep human needs of this age with vigor and vitality. *Mental health*, however, is equally critical. In a world where the pace of change is incessant, maintaining mental clarity, cognitive function, emotional groundedness and resilience is indispensable. Our ability to manage stress, maintain focus, and stay positive in the face of adversity directly influences our effectiveness as leaders. Mindfulness, dedication to learning, meditation, and emotional intelligence are tools that help us refine our mental health, ensuring we lead not only with our minds but also with our hearts. The *soul*, often overlooked in the corporate world, is the final piece of the puzzle. It is the source of our passion, our values, and our purpose. A nourished soul and spirit inspires us to lead with integrity, to pursue not just profit but purpose, and to advocate for practices that benefit not only our businesses but also our communities and the planet. Spiritual practices, such meditation, prayer, and fasting, help us connect with our deeper selves, providing the moral compass necessary to navigate the ethical implications of modern business.

Women, in particular, have a crucial role to play in this holistic concept of leadership. Our innate capacities for empathy, intuition, service and collaborative problem-solving are exactly what the business world needs to foster ethical, sustainable, and inclusive practices. By embracing and integrating our complete wellbeing into our life and work, we can pave the way for a future where businesses are not only successful but also significant forces for good. As we move through the challenges and opportunities of the 21st century, let us remember that our greatest strength lies in our wholeness, in our creating oneness. With a holistic alignment of our mind, body, and soul, both women and men can unlock their full potential, balancing their feminine and masculine qualities, to lead more effectively, ethically, and empathetically.

Laughter is the best medicine!
The power to shape our own beliefs

The journey toward wholeness, integrating mind, body, and soul, lays a solid foundation for understanding the profound connection between our emotional health and physical wellbeing. For instance, science shows proof of the negative impact of guilt on health, explaining how it disrupts cellular function and immune response to lead to chronic disease and cancer. Through my observations and research, I ascertain a clear link between emotional wellbeing and physical health, emphasizing the destructive power of guilt and negative emotions – rooted in generational, personal and societal beliefs and expectations – and the healing potential of elevated positive emotions, such as joy, love, and laughter.

Witnessing my mother's final months was a profound and moving journey, marked by a deep battle with depression and guilt, especially following my father's unexpected passing. My mother's final days were touched by moments of joy, transforming her and those around her, highlighting the intrinsic connection between emotional release and physical health: embracing joy, love, and passion can lead to profound healing and fulfillment. Joy and laughter are not just emotional states but potent therapeutic tools; hence, we need to perceive and manage our emotions, individually, in our personal and professional life, and shift our thoughts and emotions from guilt and negativity to joy, resilience, and empowerment.

We are the architects of our reality. Human beliefs, intricately tied to our emotions, are dynamic forces that shape our reality and health.

They influence our actions, relationships, and even our physiological states. Positive beliefs can have a life-affirming effect, while negative beliefs can lead to adverse health outcomes. Recognizing this, we can consciously choose beliefs that foster unity and nobility in our families, workplaces and communities, celebrating the yin and yang that exist in the world and within ourselves. We have the power to shape our beliefs, learn to see obstacles as opportunities for growth, and use our wisdom and compassion to face life's challenges. This transformation requires conscious awareness and effort, and it challenges us to become present and aware at every moment. Transforming your convictions and emotions is the pathway to a more vibrant life and a society where emotional wellbeing is prioritized as a key component of overall health.

The woman and man within us: embracing our duality

As we delve into the transformative power of our beliefs and emotions, it's essential to consider the duality of human nature, well-rooted in the medicine of the Orient and the East. Yin and yang, hot and cold, sun and moon, light and darkness, and femininity and masculinity are only a few examples of the duality in our environment acknowledged by Eastern practices, including Unani, Oriental and Ayurvedic medicine. The feminine and masculine energies exist within each of us, regardless of our gender. It is a powerful ancient wisdom that underscores the interconnectedness of all aspects of life.

As business leaders and simple humans, acknowledging the duality within us – our feminine and masculine sides – is crucial for achieving inner harmony and understanding the oneness of humanity. This understanding extends beyond mere physiological insights, touching the very essence of our being and relationships. It's about recognizing that we are a mosaic of qualities, each with its own strength and purpose, contributing to the richness of our human experience.

Whether it's navigating the complexities of interpersonal relationships or seeking emotional balance, embracing the principle of duality can enhance our empathy, enrich our relationships, and elevate our communication to realms of greater understanding and empathy between genders. As we embrace and harmonize our dual nature, we nurture and unlock a communion that promises a future where women stand tall, not just as equals, but as more spiritually connected and noble pillars of a thriving, ethical civilization.

Men and women often misinterpret each other's words and actions due to inherent psychological and physiological differences. These disparities have been studied for decades, linking brain differences to behavioral variances. My awareness of these gender-based communication differences grew as I observed interactions within my family and among my patients. It became clear that misinterpretations are common, with both men and women sometimes trapped in their perceptions, each believing they alone possess the communication truth. In relationships, these misunderstandings perpetuate patterns of discord. Whether through divorce or daily interactions at work, the failure to listen and empathize with the other's perspective leads to conflict. It seems we struggle to put ourselves in the other's shoes, especially in emotional matters, often reacting based on our past experiences or traumas. If we could detach from past experiences and be more present, communication could improve. This requires accepting and detaching from our narratives of victimhood and sorrow, which act as barriers to open, effective relationships.

Understanding and leveraging the dual nature of our beliefs and their impact on both our wellbeing and societal roles is crucial. Acknowledging the masculine and feminine within us all can lead to more empathetic, noble relationships, where communication is harmonized and elevated. This knowledge could bridge the communication gap between genders, fostering unity rather than division. In essence, our challenge is to balance the duality within ourselves to better understand and communicate with the opposite gender, allowing for more fulfilling connections and a collective advancement toward a more unified global society.

THE FIVE GEMS FOR LONGEVITY IN LIFE AND BUSINESS

Health is not merely the absence of disease but a harmonious state of complete physical, mental, emotional, spiritual and social wellbeing. Businesses have a obligatory role to play not only in the health of their employees but also in the wellbeing of the communities they serve and the planet at large. Each year our society becomes sicker and sicker, aging faster and faster. Cases of age-related chronic diseases such as heart disease, diabetes, cancer and Alzheimer's spiral ever-higher, and more and more people turn to prescription drugs as a quick-fix solution to their physical, mental, and emotional pain. As a result, individuals, families, businesses and society suffer. But it doesn't have to be this way.

As a regenerative medical specialist, I am committed to prevent, address the root causes and slow the signs of people's bodies aging, while helping the healing of their total being so they live a life full of meaning, purpose and joy while contributing with capacity to the well being of their companies and societies. To do so, I created the KHOSH MethodTM (the Joy Method). This method can help in unleashing the individual's feminine powers, also latent in organizations, towards graceful aging and joy: it is a simple six-step process, a roadmap, towards achieving your life's meaningful purpose and the happiness you deserve. The method can be applied not only to one's personal transformation but also to the transformation of businesses and corporations aspiring to be agents of positive change for society.

The KHOSH MethodTM involves addressing the wellbeing of the Five Gems of LongevityTM within you and your business. The following table outlines the basics of the Five Gems we have been endowed with while presenting some ideas and examples for you to consciously promote in your business to create wellbeing and longevity for your company, its people and yourself. Feel free to mold these ideas into relevant actions for your particular company.

THE FIVE GEMS OF LONGEVITY FOR YOU & YOUR ENTERPRISE

Spiritual Health	Physical Health	Mental Health	Emotional Health	Social Health
Meditation	Air quality	Positive thinking	Virtues: Joy, laughter, abundance, empathy,	Oneness
Consultation	Clean nontoxic environment	Learning	Sense of Purpose	Community building
Relfection	Employee rest	Meditation	Trauma Release	Service to & with Others
Honoring ancestors	Clean water	Group brain games	Detox toxic people	Career as a form of service and worship
Feminine-based Values	Organic plantbased food in cafeteria	Consultations	Relationships building	Chant / Play
Intentional Joy	Physical movement	Nutrition	Nature Exposure	Hugging
Ban Gossip	Proper ergonomics	Nature Exposure	Music/Dance	Cooking for each other
Intermittent Fasting from routine work	Access to acupuncture, massage, energy work	Encouragement	Touch/Massage	Empathy, respect and kindness toward each other
Music	Systems	Periods of Fasting from routine work	Team Building	
Practice of virtues		Music, color & aesthetics in workplace	Ban gossip	
Nature Connection		Flexible schedules		
		Conscious compassion		

Each Gem affects the other and they are all interrelated. Skipping over one Gem potentially causes health risks and jeopardizes your longevity and the prosperity of the business ecosystem you live in. For example, working only on your company's spiritual health while ignoring its physical wellness and social relationships will create stress and dysfunction; hence, compromising not only the company's longevity but also yours. And focusing on your physical health while ignoring the other Gems will cause distress in the system. The Five must be kept in balance and harmony for health, longevity, and joy, and to preserve a positive and fruitful environment at work. Your personal Gems and the business's Gems are intricately interconnected and impacted by each other. This is where the 'art' of running a business plays a role: the skill to harmonize the Five Gems within and between yourself, your employees and your company.

Adopting the principles of the Five Gems of Longevity™ and embracing feminine qualities within the organizational culture can transform businesses from within, leading to environments where creativity is nurtured, productivity is enhanced. When individuals flourish in their spiritual, physical, mental, emotional, and social wellbeing, they bring their best selves to work, driving innovation, empathy, and resilience. By fostering a workplace that values and supports the health and emotional balance of every team member, businesses can unlock unprecedented levels of engagement, satisfaction, and loyalty. Leaders, entrepreneurs, and workers have the opportunity to embrace a new paradigm – one that places human health and wellbeing at the center of business strategy. A strategy that not only drives economic success but also nurtures the human spirit, fostering a world where individual and collective can flourish and contribute to a healthier, more vibrant, and equitable world.

HEAL YOURSELF AND YOUR BUSINESS IN SIX STEPS

In an era where personal wellbeing is inextricably linked to the vitality of our workplaces, businesses, and the global community, the holistic approach to health and aging – detailed in my new book, **The Golden Gate**, and encapsulated by the transformative KHOSH Method™ – serves as a beacon of rejuvenation, regeneration, and longevity. The following steps of the KHOSH Method™ present only a guide to not only reclaiming our own health but also to healing our businesses and the world, one empowered individual at a time.

***Step One:* Reduce to Calm.** Start by cutting down on what fuels stress and inflammation in yourself and your business. This means limiting exposures to various stressors found in your diet, lifestyle practices, toxins around you, and negative mental patterns. In your organization, it means shifting your company's culture to one that discourages gossip and backbiting, competition, aggression, ego and greed. It may mean re-evaluating your company's values and choosing to create a more just value system incorporating some of the more feminine qualities. It may involve discouraging an overworking culture, or it may involve having a cafeteria that no longer provides its employees with highly processed foods. This stage involves calming the system's emergency response by steering clear of inflammatory exposures like chemical toxins, negative belief systems and emotionally toxic environments that don't serve your personal wellbeing nor the wellbeing of your enterprise.

***Step Two:* Replenish to Nourish.** It's time to fill your life and business with positivity. Surround yourself with positive influences and relationships; people and activities that feed your soul. Hire people who are aligned with your values and those of your business. Encourage feminine qualities of service, compassion, empathy, integrity, and flexibility for instance. This means being conscious about your business practices as well as your lifestyle practices. Being mindful of your physical, emotional, and spiritual nourishment and that of your business's: eat well, cherish supportive friends and family, and cultivate love, friendships and community.

***Step Three:* Release to Relieve.** On a personal level, releasing physical, emotional, and energetic burdens as well as letting go of burdens within your company can relieve system stress. Opt for detoxification and the elimination of toxins from your body, which includes following specific diets and therapies to cleanse the body and mind, allowing for relief from chronic pain and emotional stress. For your company, this may mean 'cleaning house' and releasing people and systems that no longer fit as your company adapts to create alignment to meet the needs of modern day society from an elevated perspective.

***Step Four:* Restore to Heal.** With the clutter gone, it's healing time. Focus on what systems your company or body needs to restore its function fully: think nutritious foods, restful sleep, exercise and hormone balance for your personal health. Think people with specific skills, new technologies, and systematic processes your company needs to restore its function. You may need to reinforce confidence, courage, integrity and gratitude into your company's culture. Embrace systems and therapies that encourage healing and cellular repair, setting the stage for a stronger, healthier you.

Step Five: **Regenerate to Create.** It's now time to regenerate cells and tissues to create a healthier and more youthful you. Explore cutting-edge treatments like stem cell treatments, ozone therapy, and PRP injections. This is not just about looking younger; it's about regenerating the body at a cellular level and revitalizing it from inside out. And as far as business, this is the time to be innovative, to generate new expansive bold ideas and systematic processes that culivate business growth and expansion while nurturing the wellbeing of your employees and society. Be creative. Be audacious... and trust. Create from a place where the meeting of the heart and mind finds nobility.

Step Six: **Relate to Elevate.** The final step lies in the power of connection. Building relationships and community are perfect means to elevate one's spirit while expanding your capacity. Prioritize giving back to your community. The more you and your company adopt an unconditional service oriented mindset, the more joy finds you. Find joy in service to others, which in turn nourishes your own spiritual growth and contributes to a deeper sense of purpose and vitality. And it is this meaningful purpose and joy that drives longevity – both yours and your company's.

The KHOSH Method™ integrates physical health with emotional, mental, social and spiritual wellbeing for holistic vitality and youthfulness. I invite you, woman or man, to challenge your own beliefs and perceptions and aim at self-exploration and growth; to consider how you can achieve a state of being that is noble, radiant, and elevated. By embarking on this six-step journey toward optimal health, we ignite a powerful ripple effect: healthy individuals create dynamic, resilient workplaces, drive innovation and empathy in business, and contribute to a world brimming with collective vigor and harmony. It's a vision of humanity where each individual recognizes and cultivates their inner beauty, wisdom, and power, contributing to a physically, emotionally, and spiritually healthier world, where duality is not a source of division but a foundation for unity and harmony.

CHALLENGING QUESTIONS

- Take a moment to evaluate your current state of physical, mental, emotional, and spiritual health. **Which area do you feel requires the most attention, and what are some steps you can take to address this imbalance?**
- Examine the beliefs that shape your reality. **Are there any negative perceptions holding you back from achieving your full potential?**
- Reflect on a current challenge in your professional or personal life where traditional approaches haven't yielded the desired results. **How can you apply the unique aspects of feminine energy – such as intuition, empathy, nurturing, patience, and collaboration – to find innovative solutions?** Consider specific scenarios where these qualities could lead to breakthrough outcomes.
- Consider how your work environment and practices support the holistic health of you and your colleagues. **What changes can be made to foster a more supportive, health-conscious business culture?**
- Assess how well you're balancing the Five Gems of Longevity in your own life and business practices. **Which areas are thriving, and which need more attention?** Plan actionable steps to enhance each Gem for a more balanced and fulfilling life and career.

ABOUT THE AUTHOR

Dr. Nooshin Khoshkhesal Darvish, an award-winning, internationally sought-after licensed naturopathic regenerative physician, is the founder and Chief Medical Officer of Holistique Medical Center in Bellevue, Washington. She completed her Bachelor's degree from the University of British Columbia, Vancouver, Canada prior to earning her Doctorate in Naturopathic Medicine from the internationally renowned Bastyr University in Seattle, Washington in 1995. Dr. Darvish completed a two-year residency in Naturopathic Family Medicine, has post-graduate fellowships in Integrative Cancer Therapies and Metabolic and Nutritional Medicine and is board- certified as a Diplomate in Anti-Aging Medicine.

Dr. Darvish holds an affiliate faculty position with Bastyr University, training resident physicians and medical students. She holds advanced training certifications in multiple therapies such as Regenerative and Stem Cell therapies, SOT (specific oligonucleotide therapy), Bio-identical hormone therapy, Ozone therapy, mistletoe therapy, and Platelet-rich plasma injection therapies.

The Threefold Nature of Business: Individuals, Institutions, and Communities

Iko Congo

—

HR Director | Coach

"At the heart of the learning process
[related to the task of effecting a
transformation at the level of the individual
and laying the foundations of suitable social
structures] is an inquiry into the nature
of the relationships that bind the individual,
the community, and the institutions
of society — actors on the stage of history
who have been locked in a struggle
for power throughout time.
In this context, the assumption that relations
among them will inevitably conform
to the dictates of competition, a notion that
ignores the extraordinary potential of the
human spirit, has been set aside in favor
of the more likely premise that their
harmonious interactions can foster
a civilization befitting a mature humanity."

The Universal House of Justice,
2 March 2013

Business is a harmonious blend of physical, technical, and social elements, coming together to create, offer, and exchange goods or services, thereby generating and distributing wealth among all its participants[1].

In this process, every individual in business – from owners to workers and clients – is entrusted with a deep moral responsibility. Their actions and decisions, whether directly or indirectly, promote views about what is fair, worthy, right, just, or noble. As a result, they should try to live up to their potential as *"moral agents"* and strive to **leave a positive imprint on the world**.

While having good intentions is a good starting point, it is only the beginning of the journey to make a difference and fulfill this purpose. The key question we must grapple with is: **how can business practitioners truly contribute to the betterment of the world?** It is essential to recognize that there is no singular blueprint or universal strategy for businesses to become a force for good, given that the answer to this question will be shaped by a myriad of factors like the business's size, industry, location, nature, and cultural backdrop.

But at the heart of all efforts directed towards social progress is the *generation* and *dissemination of knowledge*. Looking ahead, a vital characteristic for all future businesses will be their evolution into true **learning organizations** that engage in systematic learning processes about their role in society. Such entities will benefit from the vast expanse of existing human knowledge – spanning the realms of religion, science, philosophy, art, culture, and more – and add to it by innovating and disseminating new knowledge.

1 Business as an Institution, Henry Pratt Fairchild, American Sociological Review, Vol. 2, No. 1 (Feb. 1937), pp. 1-8 (8 pages), Published By: American Sociological Association

A fundamental principle that should shape this collective learning is the **oneness of humanity**.

Picture society as a *human body*, where each individual and organization play the role of interconnected cells and organs. Just as these elements work in unison for the wellbeing of the body, so too must we collaborate for the *holistic health* of our **global community**. And, similarly as a human being transitions from childhood to maturity, experiencing growth and transformation, humanity stands at a pivotal moment of its own evolution: it is now standing at the threshold of **maturity**.

In our interconnected world, envisioning a business as a solitary force is to misunderstand its true nature. A business must see itself as a vital component within a vast **ecosystem of social actors** – schools, NGOs, governments, local communities, individuals, families, among others. In a society governed by the principle of the oneness of humanity, all these players are engaged in a collective learning process, striving to learn about humanity's needs at this stage and determining how each can contribute to meet them.

Understanding that all these social actors influence the world and are influenced by it enables us *to go beyond a simplistic view of a business* as an independent entity which impacts the world unilaterally. Instead, the transformation of business and that of other actors can be seen as parallel and mutually reinforcing processes, both shaping and being shaped by one another.

A couple of simple illustrative examples of **this interdependency** can be useful. A business can have the noblest of aspirations of making a certain good more sustainable to protect the environment.

But if customers do not have the appropriate level of consciousness, they might not buy it[2], preferring products with other characteristics, or might purchase it but not use it in the way it was designed[3] thereby neutralizing the positive contribution the business sought to have. Typically, a business will be making a social contribution when complying with government regulations, be it for example by paying the taxes they owe[4] or upholding environment standards[5]. However, if government regulations and actions are unjust, for example oppressing a segment of a population[6], businesses can contribute to negative social effects by complying and supporting them.

These should not be seen as a marketing, product design or legal issue which one actor alone will solve, but rather as an opportunity to recognize a deeper truth: that lasting effective change emerges from the conscious and healthy *interactions* between social actors, each a protagonist in the creation of a materially and spiritually prosperous civilization.

2 For example, Nike tried to make a range of environmentally friendly shoes but these were not aligned with their customer base expectations and were discontinued https://www.askattest.com/blog/articles/sustainability-fails [Accessed on 04/02/2024]

3 A paper concludes that, despite considerable efforts and resources on business initiatives to influence consumption carbon emissions in home laundering, principally by persuading consumers to wash clothes at lower temperatures, these have not resulted in the intended level of change in consumer practice that would deliver significant emissions reductions. E. Morgan et al. 'I prefer 30º'?: Business strategies for influencing consumer laundry practices to reduce carbon emissions. / Journal of Cleaner Production 190 (2018) 234e250 https://www.pushkin.fm/wp-content/uploads/2021/08/I-prefer-30.pdf

4 "Why do tax rates and tax administration matter? To foster economic growth and development governments need sustainable sources of funding for social programs and public investments. Programs providing health, education, infrastructure, and other services are important to achieve the common goal of a prosperous, functional, and orderly society. And they require that governments raise revenues. Taxation not only pays for public goods and services; it is also a key ingredient in the social contract between citizens and the economy." https://subnational.doingbusiness.org/en/data/exploretopics/paying-taxes/why-matters

5 In 1987 the U.N. Montreal Protocol was agreed to ban CFCs and other ozone-depleting substances within a mandatory timetable and determined certain support. "Meanwhile, the companies that made these chemicals also got on board. "The industry learned how to work in harmony with the Montreal Protocol," says Zaelke. "They learned that they could innovate and create better refrigerants that have lower impact on the environment, in terms of ozone depletion and climate."" https://www.earthday.org/what-can-we-learn-from-the-montreal-protocol/ [Accessed on 04/02/2024]

6 "Hitler's Willing Business Partners" https://www.theatlantic.com/magazine/archive/2001/04/hitlers-willing-business-partners/303146/ [Accessed on 04/02/2024]; "Apple, Google, Facebook and Microsoft file opposition to Trump's travel ban," https://www.theguardian.com/technology/2017/feb/06/apple-google-facebook-microsoft-file-opposition-to-donald-trump-immigration-ban [Accessed on 04/02/2024]

Fundamental to this dynamic is the shift from *power* struggles to a culture of empowerment, where collaboration and **cooperation** among diverse social actors become paramount. Moving beyond competition and division, each entity strives to uplift, encourage, and bolster the capabilities of one another. The key to this evolution is a clear understanding of the distinct and valuable role each social actor holds.

Looking at the transformation of social reality as the result of the interactions between individuals, institutions, and communities can help businesses reflect about the different roles they can play in collaborating with other social actors. These protagonists can be described as follows:

1. **The individual** is the most basic *unit* of society; it takes initiative, seizes opportunities, forms connections and relationships with other individuals, joins with others in common service, and acts on the decisions of institutions.
2. **The institutio**n is an *entity with goals* beyond the aims of the individuals who compose, participate, work for, and run it – individuals come and go but the institution remains. It gives structure to collective endeavors, it promotes unity of vision and action among the individuals under its guidance, it allocates resources, and administers the affairs of the community it serves.
3. **The community** is the *resulting whole* that is greater than the sum of its parts (individuals and institutions). It promotes a certain culture, fosters attitudes, and cultivates patterns of thought and behavior.

One could say that in *"one given community, some institutions operate that give structure to the actions of many individuals"* and each protagonist's behavior shapes and is shaped by that of the others, each in their own sphere of existence.

Ever since I was at university, I have been on this quest, a journey of understanding, probing into how *businesses could truly contribute to a better world.* I have come across many different theories that focused on what business should do – triple bottom line, shared value, and many others. Though these models have value I eventually found in the model of the three protagonists – individuals, communities, and institutions – greater insight into what businesses should be. Businesses, I came to realize, are chameleons, embodying aspects of all three protagonists. It is not that a business is, in the strictest sense, an individual, a community, and an institution all at once. Rather, these archetypes offer a helpful lens through which to view the **multifaceted nature of business**: depending on which business relationship we are looking at, the business organization can adopt the characteristics and role of each of the different protagonists.

Let us consider a pharmaceutical company that is trying to contribute to a better world as a case in point: within the broader pharmaceutical industry and among regulators, this company steps forward as an individual – proactive, conscientious, and civic-minded, striving to uphold its duties as a responsible "corporate citizen". It engages with regulatory bodies not out of obligation, but with a voluntary spirit, eager to serve and contribute positively to the wider community.

Yet, this same entity also embodies the role of an institution, influencing and informing the medical discourse, and lending its authoritative voice to shape the decisions of healthcare professionals. It stands as a pillar in the medical community, guiding with wisdom and experience.

Within its own walls, the company can, at the same time, be seen as a community for its employees, cultivating a workplace culture according to shared values. It can empower individual initiative and collective action, where the leadership team not only makes decisions but also channels energies of the individuals and protects the community.

Therefore, for business to have any chance of learning how to contribute to a better society it will need to learn how to **transform its relationship with other social actors** and be conscious of what each relationship calls for. For instance, the mode of thinking of how a business tries to empower an administrative employee in internal initiatives by encouraging creativity and experimentation will be different to how it tries to enable contributions to the scientific discourse by promoting truth and diligence, and or how it will try to support proposals of the regulator showing care and curiosity.

Acknowledging this multifaceted nature of business enables us to see its expanded role and with it there is a need to have a world embracing vision that takes an “all things considered” approach to situations. The process of consultation can help bring to life the different perspectives of business as individual, institution and community and those of the other social actors. Through this process, each social actor, each an expert in their own right in a particular perspective of the world, can enrich the decision-making and implementation process.

Business as	An Individual	An Institution	A Community
In relation to	Some regulators within one industry	One community with many participants	Some leadership teams and many employees
Description of the role	Plays the "game"	Designs or enforces the "rules of the game"	Enables and promotes the "game"
Some practices associated with humanity's childhood that should be left behind	Selfish, disobedient, cunning, short-termism	Oppressive, negligent, manipulative	Imposing, restraining, closed-minded, forceful
Examples of business practitioners engaging in practices associated with humanity's childhood	PurduePharma consciously took dubious initiatives to exploit weaknesses in the regulatory environment to hide the risky nature of drugs they were trying to flood the market with[7]	PurduePharma developed and promoted a perspective to increase prescriptions using scientific language that persuaded doctors to prescribe a drug that was more dangerous than alternatives[8]	PurdePharma created a culture and incentives structure that shaped its workforce to believe they were doing something good by "eliminating pain" when they were actually fueling an opioid epidemic[9]
Some practices associated with humanity's maturity that should be strengthened	Generosity, Service, Creativity, Resourcefulness, Kindness	Justice, Fairness, Wisdom,	Encouragement, Tolerance, Support
Protagonist seeks to	Take disciplined initiative for the betterment of the world	Harmonize the initiative of many individuals, directing the collective effort towards a better world	Provide rich supportive unified environment geared towards the betterment of the world
Examples of business practitioners promoting practices associated with the maturity of humanity	OnePlanetGroup – "Our spirit of service is ingrained in every aspect of business"[10]	ETX – "Our story began with building a fairer stock exchange" [11]	soul.com – working in "transforming companies into communities"[12]

Table 1 – Summary of the relationships of business in the perspective of the three protagonists and examples of characteristics and practices reflective of humanity's stage of childhood and maturity

Business practitioners motivated by this vision would benefit from the observation of the business philosopher Richard De George that *"[i]t is odd that no company would think of making a serious financial commitment without extensive study, but some people think that moral judgments should be made instantaneously and require no thought, study, debate or time."*[13]

For business practitioners to master the art of cultivating and engaging with a **learning business** that grows holistically, they must broaden their horizons. This entails delving into the contributions of other social actors, learning from academic debates and striving to acquire more knowledge from diverse sources. They could take the time to volunteer with NGOs and participate in **local community** activities as well as reflecting on the role of the family in society.

7 "Because OxyContin was so powerful and potentially addictive, David Kessler told me, from a public-health standpoint "the goal should have been to sell the least dose of the drug to the smallest number of patients." But this approach was at odds with the competitive imperatives of a pharmaceutical company, he continued. So, Purdue set out to do exactly the opposite." — The Family That Built an Empire of Pain, https://www.newyorker.com/magazine/2017/10/30/the-family-that-built-an-empire-of-pain [Accessed on 04/02/2024]

8 "the crisis was initially precipitated by a shift in the culture of prescribing — a shift carefully engineered by Purdue. "If you look at the prescribing trends for all the different opioids, it's in 1996 that prescribing really takes off," Kolodny said. "It's not a coincidence. That was the year Purdue launched a multifaceted campaign that misinformed the medical community about the risks." When I asked Kolodny how much of the blame Purdue bears for the current public-health crisis, he responded, "The lion's share." — The Family That Built an Empire of Pain, https://www.newyorker.com/magazine/2017/10/30/the-family-that-built-an-empire-of-pain [Accessed on 04/02/2024]

9 "Steven May, who joined Purdue as an OxyContin sales representative in 1999, recalled, "At the time, we felt like we were doing a righteous thing." He used to tell himself, "There's millions of people in pain, and we have the solution." (May is no longer working for Purdue.) The company assembled a sales force of as many as a thousand representatives and armed them with charts showing OxyContin's benefits. May attended a three-week training session at Purdue's headquarters. At a celebratory dinner following the training, he was seated at a table with Richard Sackler. "I was blown away," he recalled. "My first impression of him was 'This is the dude that made it happen. He has a company that his family owns. I want to be him one day.' ", The Family That Built an Empire of Pain, https://www.newyorker.com/magazine/2017/10/30/the-family-that-built-an-empire-of-pain [Accessed on 04/02/2024]

10 https://www.oneplanetgroup.com/culture, [Accessed on 04/02/2024]

11 https://www.iex.io/about, [Accessed on 04/02/2024]

12 https://www.soul.com/transform-your-company-into-a-community/, [Accessed on 04/02/2024]

13 A History of Business Ethics, By Richard T. De George (2013) www.scu.edu/ethics/practicing/focusareas/business/conference/presentations/business-ethics-history.html

Furthermore, it would be crucial for them to actively participate in civic endeavors, establishing dialogue with elected representatives to participate in spaces where the *relationship between business and society* is explored.

In sum, business practitioners should explore how all individuals, institutions, and communities in society have their own contribution to make and look for synergies with their way of doing business.

CHALLENGING QUESTIONS

- What capacities does a business need to develop to strengthen its relationships with other social actors?
- What type of "citizen" should a business aspire to be and how can it be so?
- What institutional presence should a business aspire to have and which tools could it wish to develop and use?
- What characteristics does a business want to develop as a community?
- What is required to learn about these and many other related questions?

ABOUT THE AUTHOR

Originally from the Azorean islands of Portugal, Iko's upbringing has been enriched by diverse experiences, having lived in Israel, the UK, Canada, and now Angola. His view of the role of business in advancing society has been shaped by his studies in Politics, Philosophy and Management at Lancaster University, participation in seminars of the Institute of Studies for Global Prosperity and courses of the Ruhi Institute, and attendance of ebbf spaces. He has worked as a consultant for McKinsey & Company, trained as a coach and is now working as HR Director of NSDC, a large Angolan construction company. He also actively participates in grassroots activities which seek to contribute to the spiritual and material progress of local communities.

Diana Severati

It's Time for Unity

Diana Severati

—

Sustainability & Crowdfunding expert.
A change agent creating a positive impact
one campaign at time

"Our Unity is Our Strength & Diversity is Our Power."

Kamala Harris

HOW TO CREATE A POSITIVE IMPACT THROUGH CROWDFUNDING

If you are reading this book, it's because I think you are ready to be a change agent making a more meaningful impact in our world, or you are curious and would like to learn more about the subject. I am writing this chapter in order to help you to get to know better you can create a positive impact through crowdfunding and the opportunities that are available for you to engage in. I'm here to help people by giving them the right information and also to encourage them to try, because perhaps you have a project and the fear of failure is holding you back, or that you don't have the courage to dare and try. Maybe it is a matter of trust in that you have had challenges trusting other people including being confident in your own choices and decision-making process. The important thing to remember is that when you contribute to a sustainability project, to sustainable development goals, and to the betterment of society, then that is an offering made to humanity in the spirit of service. And that's what is really important. That's why I'm here and contributing my experiences as well as insights in this book. My hope for you is that as you continue to read, it will inspire and galvanize your actions with projects that are contributing to the overall fabric as well as well-being of society.

I have spent years assisting professionals and organizations to create a positive impact with their businesses. Do you have some unrealized projects? Do you dream of changing the world? Or, perhaps, you are sustainability oriented just like I am and are looking for that extra support to keep you moving in a forward momentum.

Ultimately we share the same fundamental core values. Next, I will be discussing how to create a positive impact through crowdfunding and how that can be one way of making a meaningful contribution to society.

At this point, you might be feeling those doubts and fears of failure coming into play. If I ventured to guess, you are probably reading and thinking I don't have the right knowledge, tools and even training to even consider crowdfunding. You are probably thinking "I don't know what crowdfunding is". What you don't realize is that there is an alternative to traditional financing methods.

Perhaps, you have many projects that you would like to launch but you don't know how to find the resources to fund them and to realize them. Take it from someone who has been in your shoes as I am here to tell you that you are a value-based professional and humanity desperately needs your services. The time is now for your contributions. I can tell that you are willing to move that needle to create a positive impact in our world, to make a difference with your projects and meaningful work as well as willing to create a more just and prosperous society. So, I want you to know that this is possible and achievable. Crowdfunding is a wonderful participatory and collaborative tool.

A TRANSFORMATIVE LEARNING PROCESS

My professional work is not just to provide training and consultancy. It is not the usual informative learning process, but rather a transformative learning one. My method is to serve you by accompanying you through a path of building capacity and supporting you in creating your own crowdfunding campaign.

Working with me is not where I just share some teachings and information for you to study, then expect you to go out on your own, and get it done; rather it is a process of accompaniment. Consultancy is really about accompanying you and not just telling you how to do things but inspiring you and taking you by the hand towards your success. I have spent a considerable amount of years as a certified European crowdfunding campaign trainer and consultant and the method I employ is based on transformational learning because I really believe it's not just about learning in training and putting in practice what I suggest in my consultancy, but it's rather a value-based journey built on our fundamental core values. Building TRUST in yourself, the process and in others is the key as well as the foundational element here. The process I walk you through is one that is facilitating and helping you to reach your goals. The vision I have for the realization of your project is by making your idea move from the dream state or a fearbased thought of "I am not able to possibly do that" to one of reality and filled with abounding confidence. And, I can't emphasize enough that can only manifest with a deep sense of TRUST underlying all of our decisions and actions which inevitably elevates both our professional and personal lives to the next level of transformative results.

TRUST CAN BUILD UNITY

The mechanism of crowdfunding is based on trust. Trust in buying collaboration, participation, inclusion, and trust building unity. Yes, Trust can build Unity and have a positive impact. I help organizations create a positive impact based on trust building unity. Unity is a necessary element in crowdfunding as crowdfunding is a collaborative and a participatory process. Each one of the participants, supporters of a campaign become a co-creator, and that is the beauty of it as it is aligned with higher conscious core values. That is one of the main reasons I coach entrepreneurs and businesses on crowdfunding: the requirement for unity. That's the way with which I want to contribute to a better society by implementing unity through participation, inclusion and trust. These are the vital criteria upon which a successful crowdfunding campaign will need to be built on. That is how I apply my method, a crowdfunding campaign amounts to nothing more than trust between individuals and people.

So, what exactly does this mean when put into practice? .A crowdfunding campaign needs Trust in order to be successful. The crowdfunding models I'm talking about are donation and reward-based crowdfunding because these models are the most suitable for non-profit organizations (I'm not considering the investment based models, equity and lending crowdfunding)

My hope for all those who will consider giving crowdfunding a shot is that they will conclusively become ambassadors of trust. In my journey, that is the main reason I am a passionate advocate for crowdfunding. Crowdfunding is a winning formula and tool based on TRUST THAT IS BUILDING UNITY. What the world needs more of now, more than ever before!

Coming up, I am going to share with you a few of my past experiences as well as work that I have done with some of my clients that have truly inspired me to keep going. I hope you will be moved and inspired as well!

In my coaching practice, I have supported mainly sustainability-oriented organizations as it has allowed me to successfully apply the values I champion which as mentioned earlier are Trust and Unity. With that, I ran a successful campaign for an archeological excavation, which achieved great results in the areas of receiving funding and raising the level of participation. Furthermore, the virtual cycle that descended from it was very successful because the project received a support of extra funds from the Ministry of Culture.

Some years ago, I accompanied one of my clients, the Italian National Institute of Archeology and History of Art, which was launching a campaign for an excavation in Pietrabbondante. (I searched this link in case we need more info on the project https://www.inasaroma.org/pietrabbondante/)

I got the customer in contact with a friend of the founder of the first B Corp in Italy, Nativa. We had something in common, we had the same values. B Corp are value-based entities. [INFO ON BCORP https://en.wikipedia.org/wiki/B_Corporation_(certification)] The campaign was a success, because the spirit of the campaign was shared. We all had the same values. It wasn't just a question of financing a project, of giving money for going in on the excavation, we all believed in the same values. It became a community involving campaign, because community is the core of crowdfunding and each individual participating in the project is part of it.

Participation creates unity, and I find this to be a wonderful asset of engaging in crowdfunding.

My connection with B Corp in Italy shows how connected we all are through our values and how this interconnectedness essentially builds that bridge to a thriving global community and economy. We are people sharing the same values and sharing values is a way to connect and get in touch with each other and trust is what helps these kinds of connections. It's amazing how powerful these processes can be.

Another success story is about a campaign for a book published by Viaggi e Miraggi, a Responsible Tourism Organization, made of stories from all over the world shared with relation to the countries that can be visited, and all written by emerging writers. In this book, you could read how the people supported the values of diversity, making cultural diversity a positive asset. These short stories became also an opportunity for young emerging writers to became known in Italy; it was a way of sharing cultures and fostering unity through a book. I supported this project as it was promoting diversity as a value and cultural understanding. It was really truly an amazing experience and you, too, can have the same feeling once you engage in these types of higher conscience campaigns that create more meaningful and impactful paradigm shifts in our civilization.

With all of these accounts, accountability and trust is what makes a difference.

I strive with each interaction and project I take on to tirelessly apply the principles of TRUST and ACCOUNTABILITY. These two values are guiding and propelling me in the quest to building an ever-advancing civilization in collaboration with entrepreneurs, professionals and organizations who share my vision that we are all on the path of constructing a better tomorrow as well as leave an indelible legacy behind.

The difference is not only what you do but, in the values, you share and implement in your daily work The first step is to get started! Remember, it is never too late to begin. My recommendation is that you surround yourself with a supportive community, visionaries and mentors who can accompany you every step of the way as well as have your best interests at heart. If you are ready to leave a legacy, then I know you are ready to take the initiative and dive in!

Ultimately, my purpose in being in the crowdfunding arena is for the sake of sustainability, and due to my deep concern for the well-being of our world, I am on a mission to implement all the above mentioned values in improving society. And, to galvanize readers like you into joining me in this pursuit for the greater good of all mankind.

I would like to give you a couple of tips. The first tip is: never give up. I think it's never too late to launch your project. The second one is: don't' be afraid to fail. And if you fail, the most important thing is to be able to stand up again, with new learnings. First, find the courage to dare, always. Personally, I had some doubts about working with the organization I mentioned earlier, but that is normal part of the process to wonder if you have made the right choice and if it is the right way. If you believe in the values of trust, participation, collaboration and unity, then rest assured you will trust the entire process and attract all that will align with your higher purpose.

I would also like to tell you, I'm eager to see the changes that you can bring to this world, because we can all be agents of change, and we can all make the difference in our own field/industry. That could be a small or big difference but we can all make the difference, and build trust with unity.

Everything is possible through crowdfunding as you can fund projects through trust, because you have to trust the project, trust the people promoting it and that the project will be funded. It's not only about collecting money, it's a real a matter of trust. That's what makes the difference.

It's the way to make meaningful projects happen. It's really amazing to have the chance to accomplish this. I suggest that if you are thinking about it you must try to do it because it's important and that you resonate with it. Everyone has the potential that is waiting to be unleashed. Everybody has the capacity and can contribute to the betterment of our global community by embracing and adopting the core values of Trust as well as Unity.

CHALLENGING QUESTIONS

- What are some actions you can take now to build Trust and Unity in your organization and/or professional life?
- Are there any projects/campaigns that you can identify and put on your vision board that need support? And, who can you reach out to make those projects come into realization?
- Is crowdfunding something you would like to learn more about?

ABOUT THE AUTHOR

Diana Severati is a seasoned crowdfunding and sustainability trainer, consultant and speaker with an academic background in economics. She helps professionals and organizations to create a positive impact through their projects. She has also work experiences in accounting in an insurance company and in communication in some non-profit organizations.

ebbf learning experiences?
http://ebbf.org/event/

Want to become part of this global learning community of spiritually inspired, values-based leaders exploring our contribution to a more prosperous, just and sustainable civilization?
https://www.ebbf.org/join

How can YOU contribute to a more prosperous society - in your own unique, meaningful way?

Be part of a new paradigm where your business can be a force for good, a cornerstone for a thriving, sustainable and united world. 'Ethical Business Building the Future' is your guide to rethink the status quo and become the architect of a just, equitable economy. Within these pages, explore the collective insights of entrepreneurs worldwide who have woven ethics into the tapestry of their work. Tap into the wisdom and expertise of fellow service-driven leaders around the world: in this book you will find stories and learnings from each author that offer profound understandings and practical examples on how to build ethical organizations. You can take the insights that resonate most with you and easily apply them to your professional journey.
Transform your career into a calling where every task becomes a service for the betterment of the world, blending material success with spiritual fulfillment for a work ethic that is as meaningful as it is rewarding. Step into a world where unity redefines the workplace, merging business with the human spirit.

"Ethical Business Building the Future" offers a groundbreaking vision for organizations permeated by the principle of oneness of humanity where values are the foundation of every organizational decision and action.

All of the authors are part of an organization called EBBF - a global network of industry leaders who are committed to developing our capacity to serve with excellence and improve the lives of others.
Join EBBF and become part of a proactive community shaping an altruistic, cooperative future where every individual can share responsibilities and solutions for the betterment of the world.
Learn from a community that celebrates continuous learning and finds spiritual significance in work, shaping a new ethic.

Begin your journey on **ebbf.org**

www.ingramcontent.com/pod-product-compliance
Lightning Source LLC
LaVergne TN
LVHW050927210926
848482LV00013B/559